October, 2011
Red Cross Book Fair

CHRIS MADDEN'S
GUIDE TO PERSONALIZING YOUR HOME

CHRIS MADDEN'S
GUIDE TO PERSONALIZING YOUR HOME

Simple, Beautiful Ideas
for
Every Room

BY CHRIS CASSON MADDEN

with Kevin Clark

Clarkson Potter/Publishers
New York

To Mario, Mark, Albert, Mariette, Bunny, Billy, Stephanie, Noel, Jeffrey, and Toni—great designers all—who have helped to hone my decorating sensibilities. I'm forever grateful.

Copyright © 1997 by Chris C. Madden
Illustrations copyright © 1997 by Robbin Gourley
Photographs copyright © 1997 by Alec Hemer

Published by Clarkson N. Potter, Inc., 201 East 50th Street, New York, New York 10022. Member of the Crown Publishing Group.

Random House, Inc. New York, Toronto, London, Sydney, Auckland
http://www.randomhouse.com/

CLARKSON POTTER, POTTER, and colophon are trademarks of Crown Publishers, Inc.

Design by Monika Keano

Printed in the United States of America

Library of Congress Cataloging-in-Publication Data
Madden, Chris Casson.
Chris Madden's guide to personalizing your home: simple, beautiful ideas for any room/ by Chris Casson Madden; with Kevin Clark.
Includes index
1. Interior decoration. I. Clark, Kevin, II. Title.
NK2115.M314   1997
747–dc21   97–7679
CIP
ISBN 0-609-60083-4

10 9 8 7 6 5 4 3 2 1

First Edition

acknowledgements

To my husband, Kevin, love and thanks for his many contributions to this book, and love and kisses to my sons, Patrick and Nicky, for their understanding and humor during my occasional marathon writing days. Special thanks to Kevin Clark for delivering under pressure and on time, as always. I'm grateful to Alec Hemer for his great photographs, to Robbin Gourley for her charming illustrations, and to Monika Keano for her design talents. To my assistant, Juli Grossfield: I don't know where to begin. You were great! And Kelly Carey!

I'm in awe of the team at Clarkson Potter. To my editor, Annetta Hanna, for her patience and editing skills, my thanks and warmest appreciation. Thanks also to Chip Gibson, Lauren Shakely, and Andy Martin for their invaluable advice. To Barbara Marks, whose advice and wisdom I seem to seek each day of the year, my heartfelt thanks!

And to the rest of the crew at Clarkson Potter—Jo Fagan, Debbie Koenig, Mark McCauslin, Ed Otto, Christian Red, John Son, Laurie Stark, Robin Strashun, Sean Yule, and Lauren Monchik—thanks for all your great efforts on behalf of my book.

5

*M*any of us today approach decorating with varying degrees of fear and trepidation. Perhaps it's all those glossy design magazines with their perfect living room settings staring out at us when we're in line at the grocery store, or maybe it's the Hollywood image of the interior decorator that we see in films. (Remember Franck in *Father of the Bride?*) But whether you're rearranging your living room furniture, hanging a set of botanical prints in your foyer, or just selecting new linens for your bedroom, decorating your home should be fun and satisfying. And most important, the results should reflect your personality, your loves, your life!

I believe that flexibility and individuality are key concerns when it comes to decorating. No longer do we have to begin and end with the living room or bedroom "suite." That programmed approach to decorating, so popular in our parents' time, might simplify life a bit, but it really limits our individual choices. Instead, I'm a big believer in decorating as a process of mixing and matching, or what I like to call layering. This means starting with a few items you really love, like a great sofa in the living room, and then adding other pieces of furniture, fabrics, and objects to complement that piece. Layering takes off some of the pressure to create a "total look" overnight and lets you develop simple and perhaps unexpected decorating solutions.

Over the years, I've discovered lots of wonderful ways to personalize a room by layering, and I've realized that this approach doesn't have to cost a lot of money. The key to turning a drab corner into a warm and personal space might be found at a tag sale (I discovered a great screen at a flea market that adds just the right touch of style to my living room) or even in your own attic (I found two black-and-white childhood photos of my husband and placed them in antique frames to add a cozy dimension to our bedroom). So whether or not hiring a decorator is within your budget, I'd really encourage you to take the challenge of working with what you have. You probably don't need a design overhaul—you just need to pull your home together in a fresh way!

Now, I'm not at all against designers; some of my closest friends are decorators. They can perform an incredibly useful service, and in many of my television appearances and newspaper columns, I look at what creative designers have done in homes across the country. But what I'm proposing here is that you take stock of your own preferences and then use some of the simple techniques I discuss to create a home you'll really be happy with and in. Whether you rent a city apartment or own a big house in the suburbs, you'll be discovering and developing your own individual, unique style.

Decorating your home is a lot like creating a wardrobe that works for you. How many times have you looked at your closet overflowing with clothes and said in dismay, "I have nothing to wear!" But when you pair up the right jacket with a favorite skirt or add a great new belt or scarf, an old outfit suddenly comes to life. The same thing can apply to your home, if you take what you already own and combine it with a few new or recycled pieces to create a fresh setting.

The comparison to your wardrobe applies to your home in other ways as well. If you open your closet doors, you'll probably find a general "look" emerging. There could be a lot of florals hanging there, or perhaps crisp, tailored outfits dominate; you might see a bouquet of pastels or a serene collection of cool neutrals, or there might be plenty of bright sporty colors. Similarly, if you take a look around your home, you'll notice that it does have an overall look. This might be bold and contemporary or it might be romantic and old-fashioned, but it's unlikely that you have equal amounts of both! We all have basic personality traits or preferences, and these influence our decorating just as they do almost everything else in life.

I thought it would be helpful in this book to explore these style preferences, since they're what we draw upon to personalize our homes. After looking at hundreds and hundreds of houses over the years, I've concluded that there are five basic approaches to decorating—although I realize that just as our personalities have different facets, so do our homes. See which style profile best fits you and your home:

∾ **Traditional** The traditional woman tends to prefer a classic, time-honored approach to decorating—and to life! She has a sense of history and loves the decorating styles that have evolved over the years. When she entertains, she is likely to prefer a formal dining room setting by candlelight. She loves balance and symmetry, fine antiques, classic period pieces, floral prints, and richly finished dark woods.

∾ **Contemporary** A clean, sleek, and modern look appeals to our contemporary type. Bold colors, crisp lines, and well-designed accessories and lighting are her strong points. She'll choose a great leather couch rather than an overstuffed chintz-covered sofa, polished wood floors rather than an Oriental rug, chrome and glass rather than carved mahogany, graphic art rather than a collage of antique prints—in short, nothing that reminds her of her grandmother's house.

∾ **Adventurous** The adventurous type enjoys a very eclectic look, with colors, patterns, materials, and objects from around the world, including lots of ethnic, folkloric, and artisanal pieces. She likes textured fabrics, sponged or glazed walls, old country wooden furniture, handmade pottery, and pieces with lots of character. She's comfortable with a bit of clutter, and she's not afraid to mix and match different styles and periods.

❧ **Romantic** Home is definitely a sanctuary for the romantic type. She loves to be surrounded by family mementos, fresh flowers, pastel colors, delicate prints, graceful lines, and soft fabrics. Curtains are lush and full, with lace, velvet, and trimming. Bedrooms in particular are very feminine, with framed photos, potpourri, layers of bed linens and an abundance of pillows.

❧ **Serene** The serene woman likes to spend time quietly enjoying her surroundings. Harmony and comfort are important—in life and in decorating—so you won't see bright colors or strong contrasts. Creamy neutrals, elegantly understated arrangements, green plants and lightly scented candles, uncluttered counters and tabletops—less is more!

What's great about exploring these style preferences is that they're already there at our fingertips. Whether we know, or care about, the difference between Chippendale and Regency-style chairs, we resonate to certain styles—crisp versus soft, neutrals versus colors, modern versus traditional. And making the most of our own preferences is the secret to creating a home we can be happy with. As you look through this book, you'll find dozens of ideas for each style preference that you can try in your home.

Along with this wealth of style tips for each room, I've offered some basic principles that work well in any decorating approach. These guidelines will help you as you make your choices, but remember, there are no hard-and-fast rules when it comes to personalizing your home. As the late Billy Baldwin, the dean of decorating, used to say, "The first rule of decorating is to throw out all the rules!"

In one home that I personalized on *Oprah,* for example, the husband had collected an incredible array of stuffed fish that were hanging on all four walls of the living room. Knowing what these trophies meant to him, his wife didn't want to banish them to the basement, but they dominated the room's decor! I realized that by collecting all of them on one wall by his favorite chair, we could make a handsome grouping and create a room that would reflect and satisfy both husband and wife.

For *Good Morning America,* I showed how the same dining room could be personalized in three different ways for the December holiday season. Furniture, walls, and windows remained unchanged, and yet I created three distinct looks—contemporary, traditional, and romantic—just by raiding closets and attic. This type of personalizing worked wonders on another show, too, when I gave a bathroom an entirely new look just by adding a few wedding presents and baby treasures that had been packed away in the basement. I used candy dishes as soap dishes, placed cotton swabs and toothbrushes in silver baby cups, and covered the top of an old bench in fresh terry cloth to personalize a bathroom for a woman who had just given birth to her fifth child and needed a special place to be off by herself.

Of course, in personalizing your home, you have to take into account not only your style preferences but also the realities of your life, or what I call your lifestage. Our needs, and to a lesser degree our tastes, change as our lives progress from, say, a starter apartment to a family home to an empty nest. Each lifestage calls for unique decorating options. With our first home, economics may be the most significant factor, as we are unwilling or unable to invest in expensive pieces of furniture. Still, this is the perfect time to experiment with smaller pieces like a great coffee table from an antique store or some unique pillows for the sofa.

The next lifestage is one of greater stability for many of us—marriage or a long-term relationship and, perhaps, children—and it's often accompanied by a rising standard of living. At this point in our lives, we have greater choices for decorating, yet we must also take into account the needs and preferences of other family members. Practical considerations are especially important when young children are in the house—an all-white living room, for example, may be a less than ideal choice! And in that incredibly vibrant lifestage known as the empty nest, when the children have grown and gone, we can renovate or relocate, pare down to our favorite pieces, or even start from scratch. The important thing to remember is that to be comfortable, we need homes that reflect our unique personality styles *and* our different lifestages.

We live in a fast-paced society that values disposable goods. Now, this may keep the Gross National Product counters happy, but a throwaway mentality doesn't create the sense of roots that comes from being surrounded by cherished treasures and family memorabilia. Those special mementos—the ribbon-tied letters, old photographs, dog-eared books, treasured collections, souvenirs from vacations, theater or sports events tickets, school projects, even your mother's slightly chipped bone china teacup—give your home its unique personality. They offer a glimpse into all the rich experiences of your life and distinguish your home from any other. So put your heart into these little touches!

And if you're stumped as to where to begin with personalizing, look around your rooms, attic, basement, or closets to identify or discover your own treasures. Next, decide where you want to display them and how you want to display them. I've found that once the basic pieces of furniture, lighting, and floor covering are in place, you can decide more easily where to place your favorite objects. The three basic choices are walls, where things can be hung; tabletops and other surfaces, where items can be displayed; and brackets, shelves, and memorabilia boxes that can be freestanding or mounted on the walls. Your collections will take on a whole new feel when grouped together or arranged with a bit of thought and care.

Since this book is, after all, a very personal guide to decorating, I've decided to open up my own home to you in its pages. Chapter by chapter, room by room, I share my experiences, mistakes, problems, and solutions to let you see what I've discovered about creating a home that I frankly just adore. But rest assured that my taste need not be yours. Just as there are an infinite number of ways to be a wonderful human being, there are many ways to create a warm, personal home. I should also point out that my own house will never be completely finished. It's not a stage set, it's real life! And like real life, it keeps changing and growing. I hope your home will, too.

chapter 1

THE
FOYER

The foyer, or entrance hall or vestibule, or whatever you choose to call it, is the first room that you, your family, and your guests see when entering your home. I have to admit that, yes, that old decorating adage is on target: the foyer sets the tone for the rest of the house.

The foyer can be a tricky but at the same time exciting room to decorate. It doesn't have a specific purpose, like the kitchen or bedroom, so you don't start this project with a list of essentials, like a kitchen table or a sofa. This is a space that requires ingenuity and imagination.

I found my foyer to be the most difficult space in my home to pull together. I wanted to give a hint of what was to come in the rest of my home, but the vestibule's irregular shape didn't leave many walls to work with. Not only was it tiny and disjointed but it had a funny little round window, an ugly radiator located near the front door, and doorways leading to the dining room, living room, kitchen, powder room, *and* basement!

I knew what the space required, but I just couldn't find the right furniture—above all, a table on which to toss mail, keys, sunglasses, and whatever else my family and I might need to pick up or drop as we dash in and out. Also, since I'm an inveterate collector, I wanted a place to display my growing collection of boxes. Not only do they serve as beautiful accents, but they're really a reflection of my passion for organization! Deed boxes, toolboxes, cashboxes, French lunch boxes—I've been collecting them for years, and each one represents a memory of who I was with when I discovered it. The boxes also serve as handy storage units for letters, photographs, buttons, and all the other assorted paraphernalia that seems to pile up around our house.

When I started to decorate my foyer, I knew I had my work cut out for me, but I also knew that when I was finished, I wanted a foyer that was great to walk through and that worked well: my guests could hang up their coats there, my husband would know where the mail was, and my sons could have a secret place to stash their candy.

My first task was to establish the color scheme. I decided on a neutral-toned wallpaper to lead into the other rooms. I tend to lean toward soft, creamy colors, so I knew I wouldn't tire of this wallpaper right away. Also, in this way, the foyer would not detract from whatever colors predominated in the living areas.

With two boys and a new puppy, my choice of a bare wood floor with a durable and well-anchored Oriental rug proved to be the perfect floor-covering solution. The beautiful wood adds warmth to the space, is easy to maintain, and makes my smallish foyer seem much larger. The thick Oriental rug helps to keep mud and other souvenirs from my front garden from finding their way into the house. I've also been known to layer a smaller, older rug on top of the Oriental and at a slight angle during snowstorms and downpours.

One expensive alteration my husband, Kevin, and I did decide on was the widening of our living room doorway. The spacious and graceful result was well worth the money we spent. Now I could focus my attention on finding the perfect furniture!

Because of the odd shape of the wall next to the front door, I knew I would have to be inventive in my choice of a hall table. I couldn't order a normal-size one or pick one up from a department store, and I knew I would have to remove one leg in order to fit the table over the radiator that covered a lot of this wall.

It took me two years to find a good-looking mahogany game table in a secondhand store. I brought it home, removed all four legs (they were in terrible shape), and added three legs from another table I had stored in my garage; its top was in bad condition but the Sheraton-style legs with little brass caps were perfect for the space. In addition to receiving mail, keys, and gloves, the hall table now serves as an ideal showcase for my box collection.

Across the way and directly opposite the front door is a large neoclassical mirror with two wonderful griffins, which you can't help noticing when you enter. Under the mirror I placed a stack of larger metal boxes from my ever-growing collection, providing more storage without cluttering precious space with extra furniture. These boxes, stacked from largest to smallest, sit atop an old wooden trunk. Nearby, four gilt-framed pages from an antique French astrology book, found in a secondhand bookshop, cover an

awkward wall extension where we had the foyer closet enlarged to provide more coat storage.

A nineteenth-century gentleman's shaving cabinet, my one extravagance, completes the furniture in the foyer. Not only does it provide great storage for the linens, candles, and potpourri I need for my downstairs powder room (I definitely need lots of storage space in our old house!), but with all its hidden compartments and containers, it also serves as a bar and wine cooler when we entertain. My biggest decorating challenge turned into exactly what I wanted and needed—a gracious, elegant, and functional entrance to my home.

21

the foyer

THE BASIC PRINCIPLES

Four basic principles can help guide you as you restyle or redesign your foyer.

       ~ **Traffic** Remember, there's going to be *a lot* of traffic in the foyer, so make sure you position the furniture and other pieces carefully. You should try to leave a clearance of at least twelve inches by each doorway. Carefully measure all furniture pieces that you plan to use in your foyer to make certain they won't block stairways or impede the opening and closing of doors.

       ~ **Maintenance** Although today we tend to use the back door and garage door to come in and out of our houses, the foyer is still the main entrance to your home. Easy maintenance should be a top priority in a heavily traveled entryway.

       In our house, the front door is the favored entrance for family and friends, so I selected natural wood flooring. It's durable, easily cleaned, and the wood tones add a cozy touch to the neutral color scheme. If you don't have children and dogs running in and out of your foyer, you might consider more sophisticated choices, like mosaic tile, marble, or a light-colored carpeting.

       Don't forget that if you select any type of area rug or mat for the foyer, you'll want to use a nonskid pad to anchor it. This will prevent accidents. Of

course, the foyer is the obvious spot for family and visitors to wipe their feet, so you'll want to consider the practicalities of cleaning and maintaining any rug you choose.

∾ **Storage** The wish list for every foyer, no matter how small, includes room for family and guests to store their coats, hats, gloves, scarves, and other outdoor gear. Not every foyer contains a coat closet, but a well-placed bench, chair, coat rack, umbrella stand, or shelf can be a lifesaver. As with anything else you place in your foyer, make sure that your selection does not block doors or stairways. This is a room that people zip in and out of quickly.

23

∾ **Versatility** It's a good idea to choose furniture that can serve double duty. For example, select a table that not only provides ample space for your keys and glasses but also is large enough to show off pieces from your favorite collection (this could be the place to start one!) or a grouping of framed photographs.

Look for pieces that offer extra storage, such as a cabinet or shelves. This will keep you and your foyer organized and ready to receive company at a moment's notice. For example, the nineteenth-century gentleman's shaving cabinet in my own foyer contains a roomy compartment in which I store all sorts of items, while the top can serve as a bar during a party.

CHOOSING THE PERFECT FOYER MIRROR

No matter how small or large your foyer, a mirror is an absolute must. In my home, an oversize antique mirror with its painted frame is strategically placed directly across from my front door. It fills a narrow wall space next to the staircase leading upstairs, and it reflects light back into this smallish space.

A mirror not only provides a decorative accent for your foyer but also serves as the final checkpoint before you leave home. So, when shopping for this important addition to your home's entrance, look for the following:

    ❧ **Size** Select a mirror that is large enough to provide ample reflection. Larger mirrors reflect more light into a room, creating the illusion of a brighter, more expansive area.

    ❧ **Frame** Mirror frames come in a variety of styles and finishes. Pick one that best suits your personality and the style of the furniture in your home. Or, to make a bold decorating statement, choose a mirror that is the exact opposite of what you have in the rest of your home. For example, if your house is filled with clean-lined, contemporary furniture, an overscale, ornately framed mirror can add a touch of personality and offer a nice counterpoint to the rest of your home.

    ❧ **Weight** Mirrors are usually heavier than pictures of equal size, so make sure you hang your mirror properly, using the correct materials and tools. If you do not know what to use, consult an expert at a framing store.

Creating Your Own Mirror

You've shopped and hunted through numerous stores, tag sales, garage sales, and secondhand shops, and still the perfect mirror eludes you. To create your own mirror, try one of these ideas:

Buy a piece of mirror from a glass shop, or purchase a mirror that is the right size for your needs. Take it to your favorite frame shop, select the molding you want, and have the mirror made to your specifications.

If you have a picture frame that you really like, take it to a glass shop and have the glazier insert a piece of mirror to fit the frame. Or, if you want to tackle the job yourself, have the glazier cut the mirror to fit into the frame. Then insert it yourself.

If you're handy, you can build your own mirror. Have your local lumberyard or home improvement center cut four lengths of selected molding to the desired size. If you want, they will even miter the ends. Purchase a piece of mirror cut to fit the desired size of the frame. Use carpenter's glue and small nails to attach the four sides together. After the glue has dried, you may finish the frame in any way you wish.

You can apply a simple coat of paint or varnish, or you can try your hand at any number of decorative finishes. Marbling (faux marbre), graining (faux bois), sponging, gold leaf, decoupage, and crackling are among the many options. Most crafts shops and paint stores carry packaged kits containing all the needed materials and instructions to create the finish of your choice.

Once the frame is completed, insert the mirror, and install the proper hanging implements. The end result is a perfect mirror that you have custom-designed!

the foyer

STYLE TIPS FOR YOUR FOYER

❧ **Romantic** ❧

❧ Place a vase of fresh flowers from your garden or a farm stand on your hall table. Use greenery like silver dollar eucalyptus or bear grass to make your bouquet more lush.

❧ Paint the walls in pale colors—a delicate peach, for example, or cream—as a soft backdrop.

❧ Tuck favorite photographs, postcards, and invitations into the frame of your hall mirror.

❧ Light a scented candle from time to time in your foyer. It can give the room a very special feel. Change it with the seasons. In fall, use an earthy evergreen scent. In early spring, the scent of lilac is especially welcoming.

❧ Create a still life using favorite objects from around your home. Combine a pair of baby shoes with your wedding photograph, fill a glass fishbowl with shells and starfish collected from a beach, or arrange a small pile of old books with a statuette on top.

❧ Pick a favorite passage from a book. Print it on nice paper

28

and frame it using a mat that is a color one shade darker than your wall color.

❧ **Adventurous** ❧

❧ Paint the walls of your foyer a bold shade of your favorite color—pumpkin or deep blue, perhaps—or cover them in a geometric-patterned wallpaper. Pick a pattern that's not too busy but that includes the colors you love.

❧ Add a bit of surprise by using items in unintended ways. For example, use an old cowboy boot as a vase—just insert a tall glass jar inside the boot to hold the water for the flowers. Fill an old-fashioned milk bottle with a bouquet of flowers, or fill an old tin tub with dried flowers and place it in a corner of your hall.

❧ Found objects such as shells, stones, and pinecones look fresh and pretty when grouped in the silver candy dish, cut-glass bowl, or silver tray that you received as a wedding gift.

❧ Choose a favorite photograph from a recent vacation and have it enlarged. Put it in a handsome wooden frame on your foyer wall or table. Change the picture whenever the spirit moves you.

29

✎ Place your desk in the foyer if there's space and let the room serve as both an entryway and a home office. Use attractive baskets and containers to hide your work paraphernalia.

✎ Hang your hats on a row of wooden pegs. This will make them easy to find and will add a distinctive touch to your foyer. An old hat rack also works well and offers a wonderful way to display a colorful collection of hats, umbrellas, or walking sticks.

✎ Frame maps of your favorite places to visit (past or future) in pale blue or green frames.

✎ Contemporary ✎

✎ Install innovative halogen lamps or spotlights to highlight the artwork and pieces of furniture you love.

✎ Frame your favorite family photos in different-size silver frames. Look for frames with similar, simple lines.

✎ Choose one or two favorite objects—a vase, for example, or a piece of pottery, a picture, or a sculpture—and let them take center stage by displaying them by themselves on a tabletop or shelf.

✎ Paint your walls a soft, subtle beige and paint the ceiling a lighter shade, almost a white, to lift up the room and your spirits.

∾ For drama, place a large, simply framed mirror at an angle in a corner of your foyer. The space behind the mirror will provide additional storage, and the mirror's position will help to create an illusion of spaciousness.

∾ Remember to keep artwork simple and choose one important piece instead of many pieces. The same holds true for furniture.

∾ Check your historical society or local museum for copies of some early black-and-white photographs of your town, county, or state. Choose six, place them in simple black frames, and hang them together on one wall.

∾ Traditional ∾

∾ Find a historical wallpaper that contains your signature colors and cover all the foyer walls with it. The effect will be sumptuous.

∾ Cluster family photographs in old-fashioned frames on a console or a small side table. To create a feeling of timelessness, have all the photographs converted to black-and-white or sepia.

∾ Install mahogany shelves or brackets to showcase pieces from your collection—teacups, jeweled or wooden fruit pieces, paperweights, or anything else that you feel passionate about.

31

Try to group items by color, size, shape, and material for a more uniform, symmetrical look.

∾   Use large ceramic bowls, crystal pitchers, silver carafes, or your favorite teapot to hold flowers. Be sure to insert a glass jar inside containers that cannot hold water.

∾   Hang some favorite porcelain plates in a grouping around a mirror or above a doorway to add visual interest.

∾   Use wall sconces or up-lights to create attractive lighting for your foyer. For example, a tall, leafy plant in a handsome brass container can be dramatic if it's placed in a corner with a small up-light behind it.

∾   Place a simple birdhouse on your front hall chest and add three framed "Audubon" style prints above.

∾ Serene ∾

∾   If you have the room, place a little bookcase with your favorite books (or just pile some books on the floor) beside a small chair to create a private reading nook in one corner.

∾   Convert part of your coat closet into a stereo space to house your CD player and discs. Now you can put on your favorite music as soon as you enter your house!

An awkward corner of the entrance hall is enhanced by an eclectic grouping: a collection of boxes, a photograph, a candle, and a simple orchid in a pot.

I accessorized the living room coffee table with board games, a bowl of clementines, and some of my favorite books.

∾ Leave a jigsaw puzzle out on a small table by the door. This can entertain family and guests while they are spending those inevitable moments at the doorway waiting for you.

∾ Black-and-white contrasts are lovely in a foyer. Place a collection of smooth black stones (found at a garden center) in a small white dish or ashtray and set it on your hall table.

∾ Place a single flower in each of five little identical bud vases, and line them up in a row to create a peaceful still life on your foyer table.

∾ Keep a collection of favorite letters or postcards, wrapped with raffia, ready to be read over in a quiet moment.

∾ Find one beautiful photograph or poster that moves you and have it matted and framed in a simple white wooden frame. Place it where you will see it each time you leave or enter.

chapter 2

THE
LIVING ROOM

We all wish we could spend more time in our living rooms. In the rush of our daily activities, many of us go from the bedroom to the kitchen, only to return at the end of the day to the kitchen and then back to bed. Yet the living room is making a comeback, and that makes me happy.

Our family makes a real attempt to use the living room, and not just on weekends and special occasions. It's a room for conversation, for reading, and it almost forces us to slow down. I especially love it in the fall and winter when we have a fire in the fireplace; my husband and I try to find time to sit there before dinner with a glass of wine or juice and some veggies and cheese. Many of my favorite things are in our living room—wonderful old design books piled on the coffee table, a gilt mirror over the fireplace, some special photos of the family, and one large antique screen I bought at a flea market when I was traipsing through secondhand shops and junk stores in Paris with my sister Jeanne.

Although it's not terribly large, our living room has what I consider "great bones." It's a fairly long rectangular room with three windows on either end that give us plenty of sunlight all year round. To the left of the fireplace is a small, cozy library, separated from the living room by a pair of French doors that we picked up at the lumberyard; the antique brass handles that we added make them special.

For a bit more architectural distinction, we made two structural changes to the room. We installed a deep crown molding around the entire ceiling, and we replaced a modern mantel that was out of keeping with the personality of the room. I found a terrific old mantel with lots of detail, which we installed over the slate hearth to bring instant character to the space.

By experimenting with different paints, I came up with a rich, creamy off-white in a flat eggshell finish for the walls. After they were painted, I was lucky enough to find a plaid curtain fabric that matched the walls exactly. At first I simply swagged the fabric over a pole but eventually I made simple pinch pleat curtains and hung them on a rod with rings. In combination with the wall color, these curtains create a wonderfully neutral backdrop that is airy, soft, and comforting.

Holding center court in our living room is a Sheraton-style sofa with beautiful inlays. To update it a bit, we covered it in a great greenish gray fabric flecked with gold threads. It was a big part of our furniture budget, but I'm a firm believer in finding one perfect piece for your living room, even if you have to stretch the budget a bit. The other sofa in the room is deep, down-filled, and cushiony. Draped with soft throws, it's the kind of sofa that invites you to stretch out in front of the fireplace on a cold winter's evening.

Rugs are an important anchor in a living room. Before we had children, Kevin and I had a soft, very pale pink wool carpet that we loved, but that type of rug doesn't work with small children! So after the boys were born we put down sisal carpeting. This may sound cruel and unusual, but because sisal is a little tough on the feet, it does tend to discourage wrestling in the living room. It's also the perfect neutral background for any smaller rugs that you might want to layer over it, and it works with many different styles, from contemporary to traditional to eclectic. Our sisal has been down for many, many years and still looks great—it has actually aged to a nice butterscotch tone.

Since I love to layer rugs (this is a great way to change the look of a room seasonally: roll the rugs up in the summer and put them down in the winter), we have a small Oriental rug at one end of the room and another larger one anchoring our coffee table, sofa, and two chairs in front of the fireplace. The big rug contains all the colors of our living room, including my favorite accent color, black, and it manages to hide a multitude of sins.

Our Oriental-inspired, oversize coffee table has a crackled mahogany finish that is durable enough to hold drinks and after-dinner coffee. It displays my collection of small, hand-painted boxes and serves as a great game table when we sit in front of the fireplace and play Scrabble.

I also have a good-looking old American chest with plenty of storage space for extra table linens, candles, and all those little things I need. It is flanked by two lyre-backed French chairs with their original finish; their rush seats were handsomely restored by a talented young craftsman. Rounding out the living room furniture are a few occasional tables, including a small rectangular one made of black iron with a glass top that provides a nice contrast to all the wood in the room.

Decorative elements are very important in any room, and we certainly have our share in the living room. They range from a primitive little birdhouse to some wonderful candlesticks from Venice that were turned into lamps, to a charming ashtray with a little cherub enjoying a big chocolate drink. (Even though fewer people smoke these days, special ashtrays can make great accent pieces—and fabulous soap dishes!) The screen that stands along one wall is the one I bought at the flea market in Paris. The cost of shipping it back to America was more than I paid for it, but the end result was definitely worth the expense, and the memories of that day we found it are magical.

We really use our living room. Whether it's just the two of us relaxing there with our supper on trays, or a group of ten friends gathering before dinner, it's a special place—comfortable, yet with some hints of elegance. Each room in our home plays a role in our lives, and the living room, I think, is the place where we can slow down and indulge ourselves in a little bit of luxury.

39

THE BASIC PRINCIPLES

The following guidelines will help you in designing and redecorating your living room. But as in every other room of your house, you'll want to tailor these basics to fit your own needs.

～**Placement** My long, rectangular living room has two distinct seating areas: one in front of the fireplace and the other by the windows that overlook the backyard. Consider your room's layout and then cluster your furniture to create areas for specific purposes—a conversational grouping, perhaps, or a dining spot, a library corner, or a home office–study area.

Use lighting and area rugs to establish these areas; in my living room, the large Oriental rug helps to anchor the main conversation group in front of

my fireplace. The furniture in each area should be placed close enough together to make conversation easy, yet not so close as to impede traffic. In all room arrangements, furniture should be at least eighteen inches away from any open doorway and should never interfere with the opening and closing of a door.

    Color I chose neutral colors for my living room because they calm me down and they go with my furniture; besides, people provide all the color I need in this room! These soft tones, in combination with the simplicity of the sisal carpeting, make my narrow rectangular space seem larger and definitely less awkward. When choosing your own color palette, consider your family's lifestyle. Also look at the architecture in your living room as well as its size and proportions. Darker colors will make your room seem smaller and the ceiling height lower, while lighter colors will make a smaller space appear larger and a lower ceiling seem loftier.

41

    Floor Covering The largest "canvas" in your living room, aside from its walls and ceiling, is the floor. When deciding what to cover yours with, take into consideration how the room is going to be used, who is going to use it, and how often it is going to be used.

    Be realistic: make sure that your choice is not only attractive but also viable when you take into account the various people—and perhaps animals—

who will be using it. There's nothing more contrary to a warm, welcoming living room than constant anxiety about the sort of living that actually takes place there! Even though sisal was not my first choice, it turned out to be a durable, easy-to-maintain, and good-looking floor covering that has lasted through the years. Maybe one day I'll return to that pale pink wool rug that looked so sensational, but I'm happy that what I now have works for my family. Make sure your choices do the same for you!

CHOOSING THE PERFECT SOFA

Your sofa is probably the most important piece of furniture in your living room, and it will account for a big part of your budget for this room. When you shop for this major purchase be sure to consider the following:

- **Budget** Good sofas range in price from the very affordable to the category of "this should be in a museum." Decide beforehand how much you can afford to spend on your sofa and shop within those guidelines.

- **Size** Measure your living room, the doorways in your home, the width of the hallway leading to the living room, and even the width of your front and back doors. Although size seems like an obvious consideration when shopping for a sofa, it's one of the most commonly overlooked, and avoidable, sources of trouble. Don't "eyeball" the width and length; take an extra few minutes to measure the sofa exactly.

∾ **Construction** You want a sofa that will last a very long time. Have the salesperson explain how the sofa was constructed and what materials were used for its frame, filling, and upholstery. If your children are going to bounce on it (and though I wasn't planning on this, mine do!) or if you just want to get good use

from your big purchase, you need the most solid piece you can afford. This is especially true for convertible sleep sofas.

Don't be afraid to ask questions and have salespeople explain unknown terms or expressions to you. If, for example, a sofa is described as having eight-way hand-tied construction and you don't know that this is a method of attaching the coiled springs to their eight neighbors using knotted twine—ask!

44

∽ **Style** Pick a sofa that will complement what you already own. Style and fabric choices are almost endless nowadays, so unless you're planning to start over from scratch (and few of us do!), pick a piece that will work with the other colors, patterns, and styles in your living room.

When shopping for a sofa, bring swatches, carpet pieces, cushions, Polaroids, paint chips, and any other items from home that can help you coordinate the look. Also bring any magazines or books with pictures of sofas that you especially like. Even if you don't find an exact match, you'll have a better focus on what appeals to you. If you are still unsure, ask for assistance and suggestions from salespeople, and visit furniture stores that have professional interior designers or decorators on staff.

∾ **Use** If you need a sofa big enough to seat four people, durable enough to take wear and tear from the kids, and comfortable enough to lounge on while watching television, then try not to fall in love with a tiny Louis XVI settee covered in pale pink silk! Consider how you plan to use your sofa. Will this be the main seating in the living room? Do you mostly do formal entertaining in the living room, reserving the family room for kids and TV? Will your sofa be durable enough to withstand your family's lifestyle? If you ask these questions about each sofa you consider, you'll find one to fit your lifestyle as well as your pocketbook.

HOW TO HANG A PICTURE

An important consideration when hanging pictures is the room in which they will be hung. You don't want your art to take over the room, nor should it be so understated that you never notice it. Scale is therefore important. A picture and frame that work perfectly in a small room might get lost in a large open space. In long, narrow spaces like hallways, consider hanging similarly framed pictures all along the length. The repetition of the frames helps to connect one end of the hallway to the other.

In general, using the same frame or a similar style is a great way to unify varied images. Also remember that the same shade of matting will help to unify an assorted grouping of pictures.

Even a large group of pictures can get lost if the pieces are dispersed throughout a room. For impact, consider clustering pictures together, especially if they are related in theme, color, or style. By contrast, a large horizontal picture placed over a sofa can work well alone since it's given definition by the boundaries of the furniture.

Eye level, or even lower, is generally a good rule of thumb when hanging art. People often position pictures at the upper reaches of their arms, which results in art that never really connects with the people in the room.

Remember to take into account the light that will fall on your pictures. You might want to use low-glare glass when you frame your art if you know that this will be a problem. Try to avoid hanging a picture opposite a window, since direct sunlight can damage your art.

Be creative in matching up images and frames. A black-and-white photo blown up to poster size needs only the simplest frame, but a tiny print can be made into something extraordinary by using an ornate gold frame.

47

Creating Your Own Throw Pillows

Handmade throw pillows will add character to your sofa and a personal touch to your living room. To create your own pillows, try one of these ideas:

❧ Anything that's made of fabric and can be cut will serve as a cover for a pillow. You can use the vintage fabric from your grandmother's favorite 1940s tablecloth, a worn antique rug you picked up at a tag sale, a drapery panel from your very first home, and even your prom dress to sew an assortment of toss pillows in different sizes. The nostalgic result will be colorful, functional, and very personal. Let your imagination soar. The next time you see at a tag sale a beautiful brocade jacket that doesn't quite fit, think about buying it and making it into your own special pillows.

꩜ *Create an instant pillow by placing two handkerchiefs or silk scarves (these can be purchased for pennies at garage, church and tag sales) on either side of a pillow form and knotting the corners together.*

꩜ *Purchase solid-colored pillows from a crafts shop and embellish them with pretty beads, seashells, cowrie shells, sequins, embroidery, antique buttons, lace, pieces of costume jewelry, or upholstery trim such as fringe, gimp, braid, tassels, silk rope, grommets, zippers, chain, rickrack, ribbon, or anything else that catches your fancy. You can sew these items on or attach them with a hot-glue gun.*

49

STYLE TIPS FOR YOUR LIVING ROOM

∾ **Romantic** ∾

∾ Use your fireplace mantel or a wall shelf as a "remembrance spot" in which to display cherished family photographs, children's artwork, souvenirs from a favorite vacation, or a few pieces from your prized antique toy collection. To keep this spot interesting and exciting, occasionally rearrange the objects or store some pieces away and replace them with new items.

∾ Place a small table and two chairs in front of a window or a fireplace to create an intimate dining spot for two.

∾ Make your own pomanders by inserting whole cloves into oranges, or tie cinnamon sticks together with ribbon or raffia. Then place them in a silver bowl, a wicker basket, or a porcelain container. Your room will be infused with a spicy, exotic scent, and the pomanders will look great on your coffee table or side table.

∾ Find a kitchen bowl that you love; fill it with wildflowers and place it on your coffee table.

∾ Attach an attractive old game board to the top of a small

table. Place a small ladder-back chair on either side of the table to create a game corner.

~ Find pretty boxes—I have handpainted pencil boxes from Turkey—and start a collection on your coffee table.

~ Dig out photos of grandparents or other relatives, place them in metal Victorian-style frames, and set them on a chest or table.

~ Stack wicker picnic baskets or hampers atop each other to create a unique telephone table. Add a good-looking pad and pen.

51

~ **Adventurous** ~

~ Arrange a collection of kilo weights or dried gourds in descending order on your coffee table or mantel.

~ Display a collection of great hats on a conspicuous and accessible table, shelf, mantel, or bench. When you entertain, encourage your guests to play with them as an instant icebreaker. A collection of musical instruments also works nicely.

∾ Create a hobby and games corner by placing a sturdy table
with a couple of chairs and a shelf to hold favorite family games,
such as Monopoly, Parcheesi, Battleship, Stratego, Life,
checkers, chess, or backgammon, along with materials for your
favorite hobby or crafts projects.

∾ Place casters on your larger pieces of furniture. This will
make furniture easier to move for large parties or your children's
sleepovers, to create an impromptu dance floor, or simply to
rearrange when the mood moves you.

∾ Buy or make a brightly colored throw for the back of your
sofa to add a new dash of color to the room.

∾ During the summer or whenever your fireplace is not in use,
use the hearth as a showcase for your favorite piece of sculpture,
a large basket of pinecones, a hardy green plant, or a pretty gilt-
framed mirror. It can even serve as a quirky spot for your
television.

∾ Use two complementary fabrics to make checkerboard-
patterned pillows. Add fringe in the same color as your sofa.

∾ Find a pair of handsome columns (florist shops and
home furnishings stores frequently sell them) and place your

favorite plants on them. Change the plants with the seasons.

∿ Save old ticket stubs from concerts, plays, and sporting events. Place them on a small table, and cover the table with a piece of glass cut to fit.

∿ Contemporary ∿

∿ Select decorative accessories all in the same tone or shade—perhaps a pale cream—to create a subtle and sophisticated look.

∿ In lieu of area rugs, keep your wooden floors bare and cover all of your furniture in the same fabric.

∿ Keep your mantel free of clutter except for a striking vase, a black-and-white photograph, or a piece of art. Place the object off center for a touch of visual drama.

∿ Instead of using drapes or elaborate window treatments, consider a more tailored window treatment such as Roman shades, matchstick roller shades, or plantation shutters. Or, if privacy is not an issue, keep your windows bare.

the living room

∾ Use furniture pieces that serve double duty: a low chest that can be used for storage, as a coffee table, and as a spare seat; or an oversize upholstered ottoman that can be used as a coffee table, an extra seat, a footstool, and a display stand for books and other objects.

∾ Place a small stack of birch logs artfully on the grate of your fireplace during the summer.

∾ Order an urn from a home furnishings catalog or find one at your local garden center. Fill it with silver and white Christmas balls, turning the hanging hooks down to hide them.

∾ Turn a glass-topped tray into an instant photo montage with black-and-white pictures arranged under a sheet of glass.

∾ **Traditional** ∾

∾ Cover a small round table with a cloth that complements the colors of your room and place it in a corner. The result is a great spot to serve an intimate lunch or display some favorite books and mementos; you can also create some clever storage space by placing extra items under the cloth.

∾ Select favorite photographs and have them all framed in similar gold- or silver-tone frames. Create visual interest by

54

having the photographs enlarged to different sizes. Don't forget to include one or two small round frames.

∾ Use your coffee table as a stage for your favorite collection of small objects, whether it be inlaid boxes, old cigarette boxes, miniature chairs, vintage windup toys, snow domes, magnifying glasses, or enameled snuffboxes. Arrange them to create an interesting display. If your objects are fragile, make sure they don't touch one another; this will help avoid breakage and damage to your beloved treasures.

∾ Create a formal, symmetrical tableau on your mantel or shelf by placing a pair of matching vases, topiary plants, or statuettes on either side of a clock, painting, large plate, or bowl.

∾ Create a working drinks table by placing a selection of beverages—spirits, wine, soda, or bottled water—on a silver tray or painted tole tray. For a little extra glamour, pour the liqueurs into decanters with name tags around their necks. Add a set of favorite glasses, along with an elegant ice bucket, ice tongs, cocktail shaker, corkscrew, and some cocktail stirrers— flea markets and antique stores often have an attractive and inexpensive assortment—and you have a welcoming refreshment area for friends and company.

∾ Visit your chamber of commerce and find reproductions of early postcards or prints of your town. Mat a selection in identical cream mats and display them in wooden marquetry frames.

∾ Have silhouettes made of all your family members and pets. Frame them in small black frames, tie them together in a vertical row with a red velvet ribbon, and hang them on a wall.

∾ Serene ∾

∾ Use a stack of oversize hardcover books as a decorating tool. Placed next to a favorite easy chair they create an instant library, not to mention a convenient side table on which to place a cup of tea or your reading glasses.

∾ Collect candles of various sizes all in the same color and arrange them on a handsome gold or silver metal tray. When lighted, the effect is beautiful, and if the candles are scented, the aroma is heady.

∾ Press flowers from your garden between the pages of a large book or in a flower press purchased at a crafts center. Arrange the flowers on a piece of fabric—velvet or felt is a nice choice— and frame it. Lean the piece against the wall on a shelf or hang a grouping where you can see the bounty of your garden all year.

❧ Frame three great pictures from last year's summer vacation in similar tortoiseshell or bamboo frames to add warmth to a corner table.

❧ Save a collection of oyster shells from the beach (or from a dinner out), and arrange them on a mantel or table.

❧ Arrange natural objects like pinecones, acorns, or dried pomegranates in a pretty straw basket in the center of your coffee table.

❧ Buying "good" art can be very expensive. For a fraction of the cost of a painting, you can buy beautiful black-and-white art photographs. Simply framed, nothing is more elegant!

❧ Cluster a group of glass jars, vases, and bud vases in your favorite color (cobalt blue is especially wonderful) and line them on a windowsill or mantel.

❧ Find a "butler tray" table or similarly shaped piece of furniture and display your favorite photographs on it; an especially inviting place for it is in front of a window.

THE
DINING ROOM

Dining rooms are special places in the home.
Like many families, we don't use ours every day,
but this is a room that resonates with memories
of cheerful family get-togethers, intimate candlelit
dinners with close friends, and marathon
Thanksgiving Day feasts.

My own dining room is not large, but it looks out onto a wonderful terrace that was here when we moved in. We installed two pairs of French doors where two windows had been; these doors open out onto the terrace, where we added an awning of durable dark green canvas.

In the summer we line the terrace walls with candles and have dinner al fresco on the terrace or in the dining room with the French doors open looking out toward the candlelit terrace. I feel almost as if I'm in Tuscany! (I have also discovered two ways of dealing with pesky summertime bugs: citronella candles and bug spray around the doorway.)

An old round mahogany table takes center stage in the dining room. This is an extremely practical piece for us because it has eight removable leaves and can extend almost to the length of the dining room for big holiday dinners. It's especially great for Christmas Eve dinner and for breakfast on Christmas morning.

For most of the year, the table—minus the leaves—is bracketed by four high-back chairs that have been slipcovered in many different fabrics since we have lived here. You name it, I've used it, from velvet to cotton duck! Now that the boys are a little older, I'm feeling more adventurous, so the chairs are covered in a pale green silk with cream insets, creating an overscale diamond

pattern. We keep extra chairs in the basement and I'm not afraid to mix and match them. The variety adds a festive feeling to a dining room, I think.

For an everyday centerpiece, I fill an oversized glass bowl with shells and a starfish in the summer; acorns, dried pomegranates, and artichokes for fall; and favorite ornaments at Christmastime. When I'm entertaining, I love to gather together some of my favorite small objects from around the house and place them not only at the center of the table but also scattered around it. You never know what strange or funny treasure might be sitting next to your napkin at my house!

On one wall of our dining room, a matching pair of sconces flanks a big mirror that I was fortunate enough to retrieve from my father's office in New York when he retired twenty years ago. I can remember as a little girl visiting my dad at work and being dazzled by the glamorous view of the city that was reflected in that mirror. It's a wonderful memory for me, but the mirror is also an important addition to our smallish dining room, since it increases the size of the room visually.

Beneath the mirror stands a lovely console table that's just the right size for this room. On it I placed a cluster of thick cream-colored column candles; these sit on a small black tray interspersed with miniature Venetian carnival masks that I fell in love with on the twentieth-anniversary trip my husband and I took to Venice.

Small votive candles and two candlestick lamps at either end of the console give us plenty of light from that end of the room. And since I always love to see a chandelier over the dining table, our room includes a simple chandelier with an amber-beaded shade that casts a warm, golden glow.

I've learned that a folding screen is a stylish piece for the dining room that also provides a fuss-free way to reconfigure space, and so I have an old French three-panel screen. It's the perfect accessory: its generous proportions hide an awkward corner, while at the same time providing ample storage for seasonal decorations and other items that I use only occasionally. A screen can also serve to hide a kitchen doorway during a dinner party or to provide a temporary wall when needed.

I do believe that rooms today should be multifunctional, and our dining room serves many purposes. It's a great gift-wrapping room at holiday time when piles of presents mount up. It also works well at tax time when stacks of forms and receipts are laid out across the table. And of course it offers an ample surface on which to work on the family photo album.

Don't be afraid to improvise. A good friend of mine who throws the most wonderful dinner parties once lived in an apartment without a real dining room. He solved the problem by using fabric to convert a tiny extra room into one of the most special dining rooms I've ever encountered. He covered its ceilings, walls, and two benches all in the same small-patterned fabric to create an incredibly cozy room where, with the help of lots of candles and good food, we would happily sit for hours feeling comfortably enveloped and pampered.

I also agree with the well-known designer Terence Conran, who said, "There should be a smooth transition in style, mood, and tempo from the eating room to its neighbor." It's important to me that our dining room complements the living room; the two rooms are distinctly different from each other, but there are elements that connect the two, and this makes the side-by-side rooms very compatible.

THE BASIC PRINCIPLES

∾ **Functionality** Designing your dining room is in many ways a straightforward effort. Unless you are using the room for another purpose—say, as an office or den—and you need a collapsible table, the dining room table should be placed so that everyone can sit at it comfortably and yet people can still enter and exit the room easily. Choosing a style with leaves or an extension is always a good idea if you don't need a large table all the time.

A console or sideboard will come in handy here. It can hold platters of food to be served or extra dishes and utensils needed during the meal, or it can be set up as a service counter for coffee and dessert. A simple Parsons-style table covered in a solid fabric or wool felt makes an inexpensive and easy sideboard. If your dining room will do double duty as a den or home office, keep the pieces flexible enough to be easily converted back into a dining room when the need arises.

64

     ❧ **Accessibility** No matter where you place your dining table and other furniture, you must be able to bring food into the dining room and clear it away without too much effort. Place your furniture in such a way as to keep doorways free and clear. This will prevent accidents and make serving and cleaning up much easier and more efficient. Your room layout will probably determine the furniture placement: in my square dining room, for example, placing the table right in the center of the space gives us the most practical and attractive arrangement.

     ❧ **Comfort** Even at your most formal meals, it's important that you and your guests be comfortable. I dislike brightly lit dinners, so I always recommend that lighting be placed on dimmers to create a relaxing mood. And, once again, the late great dean of decorating, Billy Baldwin, had a wonderful tip for avoiding stuffy dining rooms. Half an hour before guests arrived, he would close the dining room door, throw open the windows, and let the fresh air in. No cooking odors, just clean air, for his dining room!

Framed photographs of family and friends lend warmth to a corner of the living room.

A glass bowl filled with pinecones and pomegranates graces the mahogany dining room table.

◦ **Suitability** Before choosing dining room furniture, measure the room to see what size table will work best. Then assess the room's shape to see whether a round, square, rectangular, or oval table would be most appropriate. Round and square tables, having no definite head or foot, are considered more casual, while rectangular and oval tables lend themselves to more formal dining. My dining room required a round table to make the most efficient use of the space without causing traffic jams or awkward seating arrangements. I adore round tables, because no one is left at the far end of the action.

If your dining room can accommodate another piece, such as a hutch, sideboard, buffet, breakfront, console, or étagère, make sure that it has enough storage space for your linens, china, silverware, and other items. Also make certain that the surface area is large enough for serving.

◦ **Materials** Your dining room furniture can be made out of any material that suits your needs—and, of course, your taste and your budget. I love my mahogany table: its patina gives the room character. To add variety, I use my enormous collection of tablecloths, sheets, old textile pieces, Indian spreads and saris, tatami mats, quilts—you name it, I probably have it—to create table settings to suit different occasions. So search for furniture that will look great, wear well, clean easily, and complement the personality and architecture of your home; your accessories will add variety.

CHOOSING THE PERFECT DINING CHAIR

A tremendous variety is available in dining room chairs today. Arms, no arms, upholstered, unupholstered, benches, wing chairs, ladder-backs, banquettes, slipper chairs, wood, metal, plastic—they're all out there. But a little planning and some basic guidelines will help you find the right chair for your dining room.

෨ **Measure** Before buying your chairs, carefully measure and roughly sketch out the layout of your dining room. Indicate the size, shape, and position of your table. The standard height for a dining table is thirty inches, while the standard chair height (from the floor to the top of the seat) is eighteen inches; make sure to take into account any deviations from these sizes before purchasing furniture.

෨ **Legs** Note what type of support holds up the tabletop. Is it a pedestal, a trestle, four legs, a pair of pedestals, or an unusual support such as a triangle or a tripod? This will help you determine what style chair will work with your table. My own table has four legs and my dining room is small, so I opted for fully upholstered chairs that could fit between the legs and provide comfort, yet were armless so as not to take up too much room.

∾ **Slipcovers** Over the years I have had slipcovers made for my chairs in many different fabrics for many reasons. They give my dining room flexibility, allow for seasonal variation, accommodate family changes, and help me avoid boredom! These slipcovers can be tossed in the washing machine or sent to the dry cleaner to keep the dining room looking fresh. They make my Gemini personality happy, and they prevent spills and other accidents from ruining my chairs.

∾ **Style** Choose dining room chairs that feel great as well as look good. My upholstered chairs are really comfortable. Before you buy your chairs, test them to find a style that works for the room as well as for you. And pay attention to the chairs in your favorite restaurants. You can learn a lot from their shape, size, and style. If you're just starting out in your own home, don't worry about matching chairs; an interesting collection of chairs, if united by color, shape, or similar cushions, can add a stylish touch to an otherwise unremarkable room.

Creating a Dining Room Screen

Try one of these easy ways to make your own folding screen.

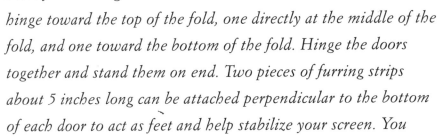

~~ *Use a set of wonderful old doors or shutters. You'll need three doors with the same dimensions (if they are not the same height and width, the result may be unsteady) and six hinges—three for each of the two folds. Any style or finish will do, but purchase hinges that are sturdy.*

Use an electric drill to create holes for the hinges. Place one hinge toward the top of the fold, one directly at the middle of the fold, and one toward the bottom of the fold. Hinge the doors together and stand them on end. Two pieces of furring strips about 5 inches long can be attached perpendicular to the bottom of each door to act as feet and help stabilize your screen. You can hinge together as many doors or shutters as you like.

Other architectural elements such as old iron gates, large windows, and sections of wrought-iron fencing can also be used, but you might want to have a professional hinge them together.

⌒ Create a mirrored screen by purchasing attractively framed full-length mirrors at a department store. Follow the instructions above to hinge the pieces together. Use wood- or metal-framed mirrors, not plastic.

⌒ Purchase a screen at a home improvement center, lumberyard, or unfinished furniture store, and finish it any way you choose. Paint, wallpaper, and decorative finishes such as sponging or rag rolling are all nice. Or for a very personal screen, try decoupage, using old greeting cards, family photos, menus, and even pretty wrapping paper.

STYLE TIPS FOR YOUR DINING ROOM

❧ **Romantic** ❧

❧ Instead of using matching china, stemware, and flatware for special occasions and holidays, mix pieces from garage sales, plates you inherited from your grandmother, and quirky items picked up from the clearance table at a department store. I once did a holiday table setting for *Good Morning America* based on the book and film *The Age of Innocence,* using old plates I'd picked up at a tag sale in Connecticut. It looked gorgeous!

❧ Place a small nosegay of your favorite flowers by each person's place setting. Use the cordial glasses from your good crystal as vases. Or do as a friend of mine does, who uses old silver baby cups as bud vases (his children are long grown). At each person's place he sets a cup containing a small rosebud and some ivy. I love it!

❧ Make your own easy slipcovers by draping a piece of sheer fabric over the entire chair. Pull it taut and knot it in the back. You can decorate the knot with ribbon, dried flowers, and any other ornament you choose.

❧ Instead of a tablecloth, use a lovely old bedspread or a

matelassé coverlet that you picked up at a flea market. You
could also use a patchwork quilt or a vintage 1930s crocheted
bedspread from your great-aunt's hope chest.

∾ If you're dining outside, drape a shawl over the back of each
woman's chair. It's a delightfully romantic touch if the evening
grows chilly.

∾ Frame your favorite restaurants' menus (the managers are
usually happy to give you one) in similar frames or shadow
boxes and hang them close together on one wall. It's a nice
reminder of splendid evenings.

∾ Make a matching set of small pillows for your dining room chair
backs. For added style, make a set of napkins in the same fabric.

∾ Adventurous ∾

∾ As guests enter your home, snap their picture
with a Polaroid camera. Tape the snapshot to
the back of each guest's chair to create a novel
place card.

∾ Cover your table with a plain white tablecloth.
Leave a different colored permanent marker by each
place setting and ask your guests to decorate the cloth

with artwork, messages, and autographs. The cloth makes a wonderful memento of a special occasion or holiday, and if you're having a celebration in honor of a friend, it's a great gift to send them—after it's cleaned, of course!

∾   Instead of the usual dinner plates, have your children paint favorite animals or scenes using the wonderful plate-painting kits that can be found at crafts shops.

∾   Create an edible centerpiece to start your meal. Place a variety of raw vegetables and fruit with different dipping sauces in a basket or a scooped-out cabbage head.

∾   For parties with a tropical theme, serve the food on large banana leaves or other big green leaves instead of the usual chinaware. Check with your florist or plant store to make certain the leaves are not poisonous! Garden shops such as Treillage in New York City sell enormous leaves from the

Philippines wrapped in packets of eight just for this purpose.

ॐ Be like the legendary designer-tastemaker Elsie de Wolfe, who threw fabulous theme parties such as scavenger hunt parties, baby parties, and mystery parties. Her one rule of entertaining: "hot, hot, hot plates!"

ॐ Contemporary ॐ

ॐ Set your table entirely in one color—white, green, red, black, or your favorite color—to make a bold design statement. A friend of mine went to a bridal shower where even the food was all white, but that might be taking it a tad far for my taste.

ॐ Get a piece of marble or granite cut to fit the top of a console. It's a surprisingly affordable way to make an ordinary piece look special.

ॐ Set your table with chargers all the same color. Layer them with mismatched dinner plates, and top with napkins the same color as the chargers.

ॐ Use an unusual material such as Mylar or nylon for a tablecloth. The high-tech result looks great at night on a table decorated with lots of clear glass balls, chunks of crystal, and flickering candles.

~ Instead of the usual dining table, create a different look by using two smaller tables—card tables with tablecloths will do the trick. This will break up a large dining party into more convivial small groups.

~ Fill a glass bowl with small floating candles and place it in the center of the table.

~ If you're like me and snap photographs of friends all year long but never give them their photographs, use these for instant place cards.

~ **Traditional** ~

~ Decorate your chandelier with greens, ribbons, dried flowers, and other objects to create a festive focal point. Hanging streamers of ribbon in a multitude of colors is a good birthday dinner idea. Make sure nothing gets too close to the light bulbs, though. In my first book, *Interior Visions,* I showcased a dining room festooned with colorful ribbons hung from the ceiling; it created a spectacular effect!

~ Tie a pretty ribbon around each napkin with a small flower and some ivy tucked inside the bow for an alternative to the traditional napkin ring.

❧ Visit the supermarket for your centerpiece. A bowl of green apples, pomegranates, nuts, and grapes surrounded by a collection of candles in different-size candlesticks is inexpensive, fast, and easy, or arrange them down the center of your table, end to end.

❧ Swag a length of boxwood or a floral garland around the perimeter of your table to create a wonderful decorative accent. Just make sure the placement of your chairs doesn't interfere with your arrangements.

❧ Write each guest's name on a wide piece of flat French

75

ribbon in your favorite color and tie it to the back of each chair for an unusual place marker.

∾ Circle your dinner plates with wreaths of different greens. Use eucalyptus, balsam, boxwood, fern, ivy, straw, grape leaves, or any other greenery you find in your garden. These natural "chargers" create memorable place settings that can be recycled into a decorative arrangement once the meal is finished.

∾ Visit a secondhand bookstore and find an old book that contains beautiful illustrations of food or of people dining. Frame an appealing selection of them—however many your space allows—in similar frames and group them on a wall in your dining room.

∾ Cut a round table in half, paint each half a creamy enamel off-white, and place the halves on opposite sides of the dining room, braced against the wall. Use them to display a collection of old cookbooks and entertaining books.

∾ Before you begin spring chores, invite your favorite gardening friends for lunch. Put a small potted flowering plant by each person's place setting, and in the center of the table, create a spring centerpiece made of gardening implements, gloves, and other things you use while gardening. Arrange these items in a large gardening hat or flower-collecting basket. Write each person's name on a leaf and hot-glue it to a packet of seeds. These place cards will make memorable souvenirs.

❧ **Serene** ❧

❧ Use fruits and vegetables, such as apples, pears, lemons, or mangoes, for place markers. Cut a slit in the top of each and slip in a small place card bearing the person's name.

❧ Shop around the gardening stores in your town for a piece of garden statuary to set in a corner of your dining room. A statue of one of the four seasons or a large finial would be especially pretty.

❧ Create a centerpiece based on a favorite book. For example, *Alice in Wonderland* could be paired with appropriate props like a pocketwatch and chain, a small porcelain rabbit and a deck of cards. Come up with a theme table. When one of my dear

friends moved to Washington, D.C., I had a "girls' luncheon"
for her at my house, and I decorated the table with books,
banners, and souvenirs of D.C.—anything related to the city I
could get my hands on!

❧ Cover the entire top of your table with favorite photographs,
postcards, or other prints and place a piece of glass or Lucite
cut to fit on top. The colorful result will remind you of favorite
times while providing a wonderful conversation piece.

❧ Cover slipper chairs with ready-made covers of white cotton
duck, available at many shops. Arrange the chairs around a

simple wooden dining room table and add as a centerpiece a glass bowl of clear glass balls. What could be more serene?

❧ Place a large ice bucket or compote bowl in the center of your table. In the summer, fill it with sand, and nestle starfish and seashells on top. In the winter, fill the container with small pine branches and top with pinecones, pomegranates, and red velvet bows.

THE
KITCHEN

The kitchen is truly the heart of most of our homes today. It has evolved from a space whose primary function was the preparation and consumption of meals to fill a wonderfully expanded role as the family gathering room and the command center for the home.

the kitchen

I have great childhood memories of times spent in the
kitchen with my large family—there were nine of us
kids, my mother and father, and the usual, and at times,
exotic, assortment of pets. The tantalizing aroma of baked
apples, apricot whip, pot roast, or fresh herbs immediately takes me back to
my Grandma Casson's kitchen, another special place where the cooking was
casual, the food was plentiful, and Grandma loved to share meals with her
family and friends. Today Kevin and I both love to cook, and preparing a
Saturday-night dinner together is one of our favorite pastimes.

Recently I had the chance to consider the many options now available
when we renovated the kitchen in our hundred-year-old house. It was a
challenging but rewarding project. The original kitchen was a collection of
smallish rooms, rather like a rabbit warren. A little laundry room, a bathroom,
and an oddly shaped kitchen that had been modernized in the 1960s were all
in desperate need of being introduced to the 1990s.

I really wanted a large galley-style kitchen that would provide ample
work space and allow for a combination dining-sitting area. The final result

is exactly what I wanted, with the modern appliances and conveniences I need, and a built-in desk where I can sit and write and plan menus for our family and friends.

An old Irish scrub pine table welcomes all who enter our kitchen. No matter how hard we use it, this table just keeps getting better with age: already enriched by several generations of experiences and memories, it immediately makes you want to sit down and relax in one of our four cozy chairs. (I've just covered them in loose slipcovers of a black-and-white mattress ticking fabric, which pulls together my mismatched chairs!)

My passion for order (remember my ever-increasing box collection?) mandated closed cabinets. I chose them rather than open shelving to ensure tidiness, and I added as many built-ins, pullouts, dividers, and special shelves as my budget allowed. Now I can store and organize the endless collections of china, pottery, and treasures that I love.

When my sons Patrick and Nicky were younger, I had a rainy-day closet filled with crayons, glue sticks, construction paper, and the like; that space now houses all the pet supplies for our puppy, Winnie.

My menu-planning area includes two large pullout file drawers and a small junk drawer that collects all the stuff—found in every American kitchen, I'm sure—that seems to miraculously multiply overnight. A closet with many cubbyholes and Shaker-style hooks completes the kitchen's organization. Since

I live with three males, I'm glad I added these catchalls. There is, as I like to remind them, a place for everything.

My kitchen still doesn't contain my two heart's desires—an island and a fireplace—but when we removed a wall and door that led to the family room, we created something I didn't expect: a new view. Now I can sit at the kitchen table and look across the family room to our back garden. Meanwhile, the large kitchen window allows us to sit and watch the world go by the front of the house. It's our very own "front porch"!

My collection of copper pots and cooking implements hangs from a wrought-iron bar I installed above the kitchen window. This arrangement allows plenty of natural light to stream in and also creates a perfect display area of my rather cumbersome collection. And lines on the pantry door measure Patrick's and Nicky's growth spurts over the years.

My kitchen is a perfect showcase for another of my favorite collections: an offbeat assortment of vintage kitchen gadgets, including potato mashers, watermelon ballers, gelatin molds, vinegar bottles, and egg beaters, that I've picked up at garage sales, flea markets, and antique stores. This is a nice way to personalize any kitchen. And these age-old cooking implements are not just attractive; they work, too!

Antique limestone floor tile in taupe and slate gray, installed in a diamond pattern, adds character to our kitchen. It's also extremely durable and doesn't require a daily mopping like so many other types of floors do. This has been a godsend with our puppy, our sons, and their assemblage of friends.

I feel that the people and food we love should take center stage in the kitchen and that everything else in the room should form a quiet, unassuming backdrop; this belief helped me choose our kitchen's colors and materials. Since I adore natural, restful hues, I chose birch cabinets finished in a pale whitewash, with shiny brass knobs to complement the look.

Other details include apricot-colored granite, called Jupirana, with some gray and black running throughout, which is used for the backsplash; it makes me happy every time I look at it. We had a friend paint all our light-switch plates and electrical outlet plates in a faux granite finish to fade into the backsplash. High-hat lamps recessed in the ceiling with dimmers and under-cabinet task lighting give us plenty of light when and where we need it.

My kitchen delights me each and every day. As I stated in my book *Kitchens,* "With my children's artwork, friends and relatives, our sons' height markings on the pantry door, a comfortable chair, our puppy's basket, and good memories of roller skating, Nerf football, early morning breakfasts, and many little heads bobbing for apples each Halloween in this room, our kitchen is surely the sweet spot in our house."

THE BASIC PRINCIPLES

Here are some guidelines to help you redesign or renovate your kitchen. It's important to do your homework before beginning any project, however. Scour decorating magazines and bookstores for pictures of kitchen designs. If you are unsure or need professional advice, as I did when I was renovating my kitchen, don't hesitate to consult a kitchen designer, an architect, a qualified general contractor, or an interior designer. These professionals can really help you to avoid potential headaches.

Layout Kitchen designers often refer to "the work triangle," a design principle that researchers came up with in the 1950s. They determined that a triangular layout is best for the stove, refrigerator, and sink, the three key food-preparation areas. My own kitchen adheres to the triangular layout, with the refrigerator at the top of the triangle and the stove and sink at the bottom corners. Although the work triangle is an ideal, not a necessity, it does make your kitchen tasks easier and more efficient by cutting down on the number of steps you need to take to accomplish them.

Before deciding where to place any appliances or built-ins in your kitchen—stove, refrigerator, microwave, oven, dishwasher, pantry, storage cabinets, cooktop, or anything else—create a simple floor plan. This will cut down on guesswork and give you a jumping-off point when you're examining your options. It's much easier to erase a few lines and reposition appliances on paper than it is once the kitchen has been installed.

 Durability The kitchen is the busiest, most utilized room in the house. Studies show that people spend more than 60 percent of their time at home in their kitchens, so when you select materials, choose carefully. Consider aesthetics as well as maintenance and durability. Hectic schedules— and whose schedule isn't hectic these days?—also require surfaces that can be quickly and easily cleaned.

My granite backsplash, for instance, is not only gorgeous to look at but also easy to clean and practically impervious to the daily workout my family gives it. Our French and Portuguese limestone floor adds pizzazz to my neutral-toned kitchen, but it also looks fine to my eyes (well, my standards

have loosened up over the years!), even when I don't have the time to wipe up after all our comings and goings.

       ∾ **Storage** Walk yourself through all the types of storage your family requires. Our lovely old house never seemed to have enough storage space for the things we seemed to accumulate, so when I began to renovate the kitchen, I carefully considered all the types of storage we needed.

       Before I purchased anything, I sat down with Kevin and the boys and we created our wish list for storage: a place to house my cookbook collection, a spot for Kevin's wine, a convenient cupboard for the boys' various projects, storage space for canned goods, and a niche for the vast number of cooking utensils and baking implements I love to pick up on my travels. And since I am a stickler for organization and a self-professed neatnik, I wanted the majority of my cupboards to have doors to avoid visual clutter.

       The final result is really practical and attractive, and I'm sure that careful planning was the key. So remember to take careful stock of your own storage needs early on.

       ∾ **Repairs** Much as we hate to admit it, appliances do break down. When I selected appliances for my kitchen I chose one brand and one brand only: General Electric's Monogram line (the glass panels came in my favorite accent color, black). I stayed with GE so that if and when something broke down or I had a question, I could call one manufacturer rather than many. Busy lives require easy and direct solutions to the problem of repairs. So when you shop for appliances for your kitchen, carefully consider using one manufacturer for as many items as possible. This may save you hassles, too.

CHOOSING THE PERFECT KITCHEN TABLE

It took me a long time to find the perfect kitchen table, the kind that beckons you to come over and sit down as soon as you enter the room. It was an important decision, I knew: the table had to be big enough to accommodate family and friends, sturdy enough to withstand bags of groceries waiting to be put away, durable enough to take the daily barrage of meals, homework, and other activities, and attractive enough to enhance the look of our kitchen.

Finding the right table seemed to be a formidable task, but it doesn't have to be. When you shop for this multipurpose piece of furniture, consider the following:

~ **Size** Select a table that will seat your family comfortably at mealtime as well as provide ample space for the various other activities you perform in the kitchen. A table that can be expanded with leaves is great if you have the room for it. Be sure to measure your kitchen to determine how large a table the room can accommodate, while still leaving room for traffic.

~ **Style** Choose a table that suits your lifestyle. A house filled with children might be best served by an old Irish scrub pine table like mine; no matter how much of a beating it takes, it will still look great. The table should also blend in with the rest of your kitchen. A farmhouse table works well in a country kitchen, while a granite-topped metal table would look terrific in a loft-style space.

~ **Function** Don't forget the functional aspects of the kitchen table. My old pine table has drawers, which I find invaluable as extra storage space for napkins, candles, and even pencils and erasers for when the boys do their homework at the table. And as is often the case with antique furniture, the more wear and tear it takes, the more character it gains!

I do, however, sometimes find myself looking longingly at the smooth Formica-type tabletops of many of my friends. For them, spilled cereal or errant red wine doesn't present the clean-up problems that I have. As with any decorating choice you make, the only right one is the one that works for you and your family.

Creating Your Own Message Center

Even in our e-mail world, there is still no more efficient way to get messages to your family than through a home message center. Every kitchen should have a spot where phone messages can be posted, shopping lists tacked up, important meetings and appointments noted, and special occasions announced.

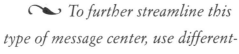 *Purchase a large blackboard or a cork bulletin board, and hang it in a spot where it will be in view. Make certain to have plenty of chalk available for the blackboard and pushpins, paper, and pens for the bulletin board.*

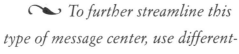 *To further streamline this type of message center, use different-colored chalk or pieces of paper to signify different types of messages—blue for telephone calls, yellow for appointments and meetings, pink for shopping lists, and so forth.*

~ Create your own fabric-covered message center, starting with a large piece of sturdy plywood. Select any size you wish; a nice size is 2 feet by 3 feet. Cover the board with polyester batting, which can be found in a fabric store. Attach the batting to the plywood with glue or a staple gun. Then pick an attractive and sturdy fabric; you will need about a yard and a quarter with a minimum width of 48 inches.

Cover the board with the fabric and fold it back around the edges as if you were wrapping a package. Attach the flaps to the back of the board with glue, staples, or thumbtacks. Purchase twenty yards of pretty flat ribbon, braid, or cord; flat satin ribbon approximately one-quarter inch wide works well. Create a trellis pattern on the fabric side of your message center, and use thumbtacks to secure the ends of the ribbon to the back of the board. Tuck letters, invitations, notes, and lists under the ribbons to create a great message center.

the kitchen

STYLE TIPS FOR YOUR KITCHEN

❧ Romantic ❧

❧ Search for some old silver napkin rings at flea markets. They look wonderful on your table, and they can create a stunning still life on a shelf or windowsill with other small silver pieces.

❧ For a pretty message center, paint the edges of a bulletin board with an ivy motif.

❧ Pin up favorite greeting cards, postcards, inspirational messages, and mementos on your bulletin board.

❧ Use a pretty dish towel, a favorite piece of lace, or a bit of old linen as a simple café curtain.

❧ Display some of your favorite objects on a shelf where you can see them every day.

❧ An old tablecloth from the forties or fifties—the type you can usually find in abundance at tag sales—will make great seat cushions, especially if you have mismatched kitchen chairs. Look for fabric with wonderful fruit and vegetable motifs.

❧ Use a favorite kitchen item, such as your grandmother's old coffee pot, as a vase. Place it in the center of your kitchen table.

❧ An antique bowl can be the perfect, unexpected container

for an assortment of fresh fruit and will make a good-looking centerpiece for your kitchen table.

෴ Keep copies of your favorite recipes rolled up and tied with a piece of ribbon or bit of raffia in a basket on your countertop. In this way, when someone asks for a recipe or comments on your fabulous baking, you can share with ease!

෴ A quilt from your bedroom can dress up the plainest kitchen when hung on a wall or over your table. Be sure to coat it with a stain-resistant spray first.

෴ Adventurous ෴

෴ Select black-and-white vinyl squares to give your kitchen a checkerboard floor. Consider laying the squares on the diagonal to increase the appearance of space in the room.

෴ Turn a windowsill into an indoor herb garden with small terra-cotta pots and seedling plants (growing from seed takes forever!) to give you and your family fresh herbs all year round.

Remember to snip not only for your salads, but also your soups, sauces, and roasts.

∾   Store flour, sugar, rice, and other staples in large clear glass Mason jars and place them along the back of your countertop.

∾   Use texture to give your kitchen personality—consider granite for the countertops, burnished metal for the cabinets, old pulls for handles, and antique brick for the floor.

∾   Leave your windows unadorned. If you need privacy, install shades that can be raised during the day, or use wooden shutters that can be folded back.

∾   Line up a few mortar-and-pestles of varying heights on a windowsill to create a wonderfully functional tableau.

∾   Hang three small children's chairs on a blank wall. Not only do they add architectural detail to an empty space but they come in handy when you have little visitors.

∾   Why not create your own masterpiece by tiling the countertop in a durable colorful tile?

∾   Store flavored oils, jellies, or other bottled foods in antique bottles. Line them up along the countertop as decorative accents. They can also be turned into instant gifts for friends!

Strategically and lovingly placed pillows add glamour to the bed in our master bedroom.

My bedroom desk is a depository for some of my favorite things.

❧ **Contemporary** ❧

❧ Blow up four of your favorite family photographs to poster size, frame them in black or white, and create your own art gallery along a blank wall.

❧ Simplify clutter by investing in specialty storage for your small appliances and countertop items. Such items as spice racks, canisters, tray slides, lazy Susans, and appliance garages will help you keep your countertops sleek-looking.

❧ Store your spatulas, whisks, and big spoons in simple tubular vases. Look for vases made of relatively thick glass.

❧ Hang a restaurant-style steel pot rack from your ceiling or wall to create efficient storage.

97

~ Choose materials in the same color palette to create a unified look. Consider pale woods, limestone, and acid-washed marble.

~ Run some coated wire shelving around the perimeter of your kitchen, about a foot from the ceiling, as a storage place for larger items.

~ Set up a couple of labeled baskets to hold coupons, recipes, mail, gloves, and other objects that can otherwise clutter up countertops and tables.

~ Cover your chairs with loose slipcovers made of washable cotton duck or mattress ticking for a clean look.

~ Traditional ~

~ Create your own herb-drying rack by installing a wooden dowel or broom handle over a window or by suspending it from the ceiling. Tie on your favorite fresh herbs with raffia or string so that they'll always be available when you need them.

~ Collect old wooden game boards like backgammon and Parcheesi boards and hang them along one wall. You might even pick up one of the deeper colors in the boards to paint your window trim.

~ Start collecting old bottles and fill them with pretty colored water. Peel a continuous rind of lemon and add it to the bottle along with a sprig of rosemary or any other favorite herb. Cap it with an old wine cork, tie a bit of raffia around the bottle, and display it on a counter or on a glass shelf in front of a window to catch the sun's rays.

∾ Hang a piece of Peg-Board with hooks near your stove to hold kitchen gadgets. This makes the utensils easy to find while you are cooking and creates a decorative effect.

∾ Use an old farmhouse table or a butcher block as an island for food preparation.

∾ A favorite dresser or chest can work well for dish storage; you can always paint a new dresser using a textured effect to make it look old.

∾ Buy a sturdy wooden ladder at a hardware store and place it in a corner of your kitchen. It will make a terrific plant stand, cookbook shelf, towel rack, or display unit, and it will really come in handy when you need to reach that turkey platter on the highest shelf in your kitchen.

∾ A large school blackboard mounted on a wall is a great place to keep your food list, with family photographs tucked around the edges.

the kitchen

❧ Serene ❧

❧ Place a small easy chair in your kitchen. This will be the perfect spot to relax with a cup of tea, to look over a favorite recipe, or to welcome a friend to keep you company while you putter around the kitchen.

❧ Use unlikely kitchen pieces, like a tiered dining server or a semainier (a tall narrow seven-drawer cupboard) to organize your kitchen goods. If you find an old, damaged piece, consider glazing it a vibrant green or deep red.

❧ Find the smallest CD player available (Sony makes a great one) and treat yourself to discs of ten of your favorite musicians. This way you'll always have music in your kitchen.

❧ Decide on a color you love, and when you shop at flea markets, tag sales, and antique shops, keep your eyes open for a variety of old metal trays—round, square, rectangular, and whimsical—from the 1940s and 1950s. Stand them along a counter or hang them on a wall for great effect.

❧ Keep a few of your favorite books—gardening, poetry, and fiction, *not* just cookbooks—in the kitchen. Leaf through them occasionally to create little moments of private time. But make sure to store the books away from heat, steam, and grease.

◡ Use a beautiful tile as a trivet or place it in the center of your stovetop for a spoon rest.

◡ Instead of using the commercial plastic bottle, fill a small glass oil or vinegar cruet with dishwashing liquid and place it by your sink. This is especially nice if your preferred detergent comes in a pretty color.

101

◡ Rest your sink-side sponges and dish scrubbers on a favorite small dish or in a simple glass bowl.

◡ Keep a clear glass bowl full of fruit. Green apples or lemons and limes add gentle color and fragrance to any kitchen.

THE
BEDROOM

*Our busy days come to a rest when we
finally close our bedroom door at night. It is
here that we can relax and reflect on (or forget)
the day's events, and begin the process of
regeneration and rejuvenation for the next day.
The bedroom soothes our souls.*

When I first saw the master bedroom in our house, it was love at first sight. It was at least twice as large as our apartment bedroom (which, to be perfectly honest, was tiny!), it had lots of natural light, and best of all, it had a fireplace.

Now, a fireplace is great not just because it's romantic and cozy, but also because it creates a focal point for decorating. Our fireplace stands opposite our bed and is the first thing I see in the morning. This prompted me to paint a favorite phrase from Katharine Hepburn's autobiography in the very softest shade of beige on the white mantel: "Embrace life." It's barely noticeable, but I'm happy it's there.

Also on the mantel are two pictures in silver frames that were given to us by Nicky and Patrick's godmother, Kathy Johnson, when our sons were born. The frames are engraved with each boy's weight, height, date, and time of birth. Two Victorian metal frames, found at a flea market, hold photographs (converted into black-and-white prints) of my husband and me when we were children.

The boxed radiator cover, which is painted the same color as our walls, also holds an array of framed family photographs taken at weddings, parties, and other family gatherings over the years. These are some of the personal touches that really make our bedroom cozy.

I decided on very soft, neutral colors in the bedroom, as in the rest of the house, and so a wonderful muted cream color with just a hint of peach was my choice for all the walls and millwork. I also wanted an unfussy window treatment, so I chose a crisp, tailored Roman shade made from a material that resembles old Chinese silk. It's very close to the shade of the walls and cabinets, it has a magnificent texture, and if you look carefully, you can see the pattern of a flower subtly woven throughout the fabric.

Also like the rest of the house, our bedroom is a mixture of objects that represent different places and times in my life. For instance, our cold-rolled steel bed was designed and built for us by my very talented sister Mary and my brother-in-law, Ron Lessard. To enhance the shape and finish of the bed, which has a wonderful copper patina and strong straight lines, I deliberately kept all the bed linens soft and light in a neutral shade of peach. A thin-striped bed skirt in shades of peach and white with inverted pleat edges gives a tailored, neat appearance.

I love to change my rooms with the seasons, so during the winter the bed is topped with a matelassé coverlet I bought at the Paris flea market on that shopping excursion with my sister Jeanne. A big, fluffy down-filled duvet rests at the foot of the bed; it's covered in a soft beige

with a simple vine pattern embroidered on the edge in white.

And since I believe you can never have too many pillows on your bed—sometimes Kevin just looks at our collection and laughs—we have two 26-inch-square European shams (great for reading in bed) in the same peachy pattern as the duvet, plus four pillows for sleeping, and a little boudoir pillow or neck roll that I change periodically. I read somewhere that we spend seven years of our life in bed, so I splurged on our sheets—they're as soft as can be. Remember: the higher the thread count, the finer the feel.

At the foot of the bed is a small upholstered bench, which serves as a good spot to toss the pillows and the bed linens we don't need for sleeping. Above the bed hang two pictures of Venice. The modern lamps on either side of the bed lend a little contrast to the Old World feel of these prints. And instead of a predictable night table, I have a Japanese futon chest from the 1930s by my side of the bed. Frankly, it's the best night table I've ever had because there's plenty of room on top for my mystery novels, telephone, notepad, framed family photos, and alarm clock.

Even though our bedroom is not huge, we do have room for a small love seat. I also picked up a boudoir chair at a local flea market and paired it with a little ottoman. These three pieces—the love seat, ottoman, and boudoir chair—are covered in a dove-brown chenille that helps pull them together. This is something to keep in mind if you have too many mismatched pieces, or if you want to create a more serene look in your bedroom: choose one or two fabrics to cover all furniture. A kilim pillow adds just the right touch to the love seat, and to complete the look I layered an old Oriental rug on top of the light Berber wool carpet that covers the floor.

A four-foot-high jewelry chest helps keep my scarves and jewelry organized. I know it sounds like a luxury, but I think this is an essential bedroom item for most women, because accessories get so jumbled when there isn't the space to properly organize and store them. If you find an old chest or cupboard with lots of compartments, you might want to try the same idea. My

most recent purchase is a two-tiered table made of glass and wrought iron. This clean-lined piece from Crate & Barrel stylishly organizes my huge collection of magazines.

Soft colors and textures, cherished mementos, and *lots* of organization make my bedroom a practical refuge!

THE BASIC PRINCIPLES

Bedrooms have become noticeably more comfortable over the past decade.

Draped beds, soft fabrics, plush chairs, loads of pillows, photographs of family and friends, and a plethora of decorative details all work toward creating an intimate atmosphere tinged with a sense of personal style and occasionally drama. Here are some basic concepts to keep in mind when you begin to decorate your bedroom.

◦ **Comfort** The bed is obviously the basic design element in the bedroom. Your floor plan should allow room for easy access to and around the bed. If you enjoy fresh air, position your bed to take full advantage of an open window. If your sleep is disturbed by early morning light, why not install room-darkening shades or blackout curtains and drapes? If you like to sit in your room and talk over the day's events with your family before you go to sleep, as Kevin and I do, be sure to have a spot for people to sit in addition to your bed, unless you like everyone to pile on your bed! Remember that comfort is your number one priority when designing your bedroom.

◦ **Clothing Storage** Most of our clothing is typically stored in our bedrooms, so make sure that your closets and storage pieces are adequate for your needs. Kevin and I have a pair of seven-drawer chests that flank the fireplace. Tall and narrow, they don't take up too much floor space, but they expand the storage space offered by our built-in closets. If you live in a house that has little or no closet space, you'll want to invest in a freestanding piece, like a large armoire, cupboard, clothespress, or tall cabinet, in which to store your clothes. Smaller boxes help keep accessories and jewelry well organized.

    ∾ **Adaptability** When decorating a child's bedroom, keep in mind that this room will need to change over time. Most thirteen-year-olds don't want Humpty Dumpty wallpaper or a tiny dresser with Little Bo-peep decals. In fact, my son Nicky has just told me he no longer wants his whole room outfitted like Yankee Stadium! Regardless of age, the furnishings and decoration for a child's bedroom should allow him or her to play, entertain friends, study, listen to music, and just hang out. A glass-fronted memorabilia box and large poster frames helped Nicky organize all his favorite sports treasures and paraphernalia.

109

    ∾ **Lighting** I recently invested a bit of time and money to have five high-hats, or recessed lights, installed in our bedroom ceiling. A dimmer controls the lighting, allowing different intensities, which makes a big difference. When deciding on your own bedroom lighting, try to use a variety of sources, including overhead lights, a table or floor lamp, and bed lights for reading. Swing-arm lamps attached to the wall are a great solution for nighttime reading, since they don't take up space on a night table.

∾ **Privacy** If a bedroom is shared, whether by siblings or spouses, some sense of personal space should be established for each person. A favorite chair, a chest of drawers, or even a shelf can be all that's needed to provide a bit of privacy. In my bedroom, my night table is my personal domain: I know that whatever I slip into it will be there the next night when I return.

CHOOSING THE PERFECT CHEST OF DRAWERS

Before you buy a dresser, chest of drawers, armoire, or any other piece of furniture designed for storage, take the time to examine your needs.

∾ **Assess** Ask yourself these questions:

Do I need to store everything in my bedroom, or can I store seasonal items elsewhere in the house or at the dry cleaners?

Do I really need everything I'm trying to fit into my bedroom?

Do most of my clothes need to be stored on hangers, or can they be folded and placed on shelves or in drawers?

Is my bedroom large enough to hold a big piece of furniture such as a triple dresser or an armoire?

Do I already own something in another room that could be used for storage?

And, most important, what is my budget for this purchase?

Now take a look at the other furniture in your bedroom. Is it traditional or contemporary? What colors predominate?

꙳ **Shop** Once you have answered these basic questions, take swatches of your bedroom fabrics and Polaroids of your other furniture pieces, and start exploring department stores, furniture stores, auctions, thrift shops, tag sales, flea markets, garage sales, and antique stores. Don't forget to look in your attic, basement, garage, and the other rooms in your house. Sometimes a large trunk from your attic can create a whole new look for your bedroom.

꙳ **Refinish** If you find the perfect chest of drawers but it's the wrong finish or has the ugliest hardware you've ever seen, don't despair. Try to look beyond the surface finish and examine the shape, scale, proportion, and style of the piece. A little paint and some good-looking knobs from a home improvement center or hardware store can turn a fifteen-dollar garage-sale reject into a rejuvenated treasure.

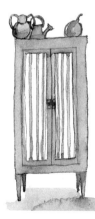

Creating an Organized Closet

An unorganized closet is a real nuisance when you are trying to rush out the door. Try some of these ideas to help bring calm to your bedroom closet.

There comes a time when you simply have to prune your wardrobe. Here's a rule of thumb: If you haven't worn it in a year, get rid of it. The space you gain will be worth the pain of parting with unworn clothes. Of course, if something really means a lot to you—your prom dress, your wedding dress, your child's christening outfit—store it.

Closet shelves are usually too shallow and high to store socks, underwear, sweaters, scarves, hats, gloves, and extra blankets. Instead, use boxes, plastic bins, baskets, hatboxes, shoe boxes, or any other container that will keep your clothing organized in your closet. Don't forget to label each box with its contents in big

Copper pots become an instant kitchen "curtain" alongside our family message center, an old blackboard.

Simple glass jars and a black-and-white framed photo add style to the bathroom.

letters. A great way to organize shoes is to store them in their original boxes. Take a Polaroid of each pair and tape it to the end of the box for instant identification.

A light in the closet is a little luxury that no one can afford to be without. If you don't have a light source in the closet and don't want to have an electrician install one, buy an inexpensive battery-operated light at a hardware or home improvement store. These can be attached simply to the ceiling or wall of your closet. Just be sure plastic cleaning bags never get near the source of light.

In dire situations, see if you can afford to have your closet professionally organized or have a closet organization system installed. To locate one of these services, check the Yellow Pages, ask your friends for referrals, check with the Chamber of Commerce, or look for ads in the newspaper or Pennysaver.

the bedroom

STYLE TIPS FOR YOUR BEDROOM

❧ **Romantic** ❧

❧ Hang a trio of favorite family hats on the back of your bedroom door.

❧ Use a vintage tablecloth from a flea market or antique shop as a striking coverlet for your bed.

❧ In lieu of the standard night table, place a tea table next to your bed. It can do double duty as a place for an intimate breakfast for two if you add a chair.

❧ If you don't have a four-poster bed, you can create the look of one by hanging a mosquito-net canopy from a ceiling hook and draping it over your bed. Hooks and nets are available through many mail-order catalogs and from stores like Ikea, Crate & Barrel, and Pottery Barn.

❧ Another creative idea is to cut four rods the length and width of your bed and suspend them from your ceiling. Hang simple pocket-rod drapes or tab curtains from the rods and you have an instant four-poster.

❧ Buy some calligraphy pens and try your hand at writing a favorite thought to start your day. Frame it in an inexpensive small frame, place it on your night table and remember to look at it often. (And change it, too!)

ॐ Children's (your own or friends') handmade creations are great paperweights for your nighttime reading.

ॐ Start a collection—magnifying glasses, old cameras, whatever appeals to you—and display on a windowsill.

ॐ Tie bouquets of your favorite dried flowers to the bedposts with a pretty piece of ribbon.

ॐ Create a unique shade for a plain store-bought lamp by using old sheets of music or pages from a vintage illustrated book to assemble a decoupage.

ॐ Hang a handsome old pair of iron gates on the wall for a headboard.

ॐ Line up a collection of starfish and cowrie shells on a windowsill.

ॐ Adventurous ॐ

ॐ Try placing your bed on angle in a corner of your room instead of the usual 90-degree against-the-wall configuration.

ॐ Use vintage or retro-style linens on the bed. Pick an era—forties floral, say, or sixties pop—and then mix and match.

꙳ Instead of the usual headboard, install a shelf the width of your bed, using attractive brackets and making sure to leave yourself ample headroom. Fill it with books and pieces from your favorite collection. Make sure you have plenty of light for bedtime reading.

꙳ A small child's chair can nicely hold a stuffed animal from your childhood.

꙳ For a bit of drama, find a chandelier that would normally be used in an entranceway or dining room and hang it directly above your bed. Make sure to place it on dimmers.

꙳ Stencil a favorite saying, pattern, or a passage from a book around the perimeter of your room, just beneath the ceiling, or as I did, on the fireplace mantel.

꙳ Take an old but still functional lamp from your living room and move it to your bedroom to cast a fresh light in the room.

꙳ Paint (or hire a local art student) your family tree on a plain wall.

the bedroom

∾ Contemporary ∾

∾ Instead of table lamps, install sconces above your night tables. This will free up the surface area and provide a higher light for more comfortable reading.

∾ Install a master control switch for the lights, television, stereo, and drapery control next to your bed. Now you can control the entire room setting from this spot.

∾ Pad the wall behind your bed and leave off the headboard. It will be a more comfortable solution if you enjoy reading in bed.

∾ Instead of the typical lighting used in bedrooms, install halogen track lighting. The architectural lines of the light fixture and the lightbulbs themselves will add a bit of architectural interest.

∾ A small footstool next to your bed is a fresh way to hold phone, pad, and pens.

∾ Use sleek office storage units—flat files, file cabinets, storage lockers, and rolling files—for your clothing storage instead of the traditional chest of drawers or triple dresser.

∾ If you have an unsightly radiator, build or buy a box cover, paint it the same color as your walls, and use it as an instant photo gallery.

117

the bedroom

❧ Traditional ❧

❧ Place a small love seat or ottoman at the foot of the bed. It makes a great spot to hold extra duvets, throws, and pillows while you are sleeping.

❧ A simple white tulle fabric that is draped across the head of the bed from the ceiling to the floor can be held in place with two Shaker pegs.

❧ Buy simple white cotton decorative pillows and with a fabric pen handwrite your favorite sayings. Place three on your bed or easy chair.

❧ A favorite goblet filled with a single flower won't break your budget and is a wonderful view to wake up to when placed on your nightstand.

❧ An old door mounted sideways on the wall makes a dramatic headboard.

❧ A mismatched set of three or four china dishes (or favorite ones that you don't use anymore) can be placed on platestands to add a colorful touch to a windowsill, mantel, shelf, or radiator cover.

❧ Place small sachets between your box spring and mattress to infuse your bedroom with your favorite scent.

∾ Attach a tassel to your bedside lamp switch to give it a little character.

∾ Hang a pair of your favorite drapes, a large tapestry, an antique patchwork quilt, or an area rug at the head of your bed for an unusual headboard.

∾ Place a chair next to your bed to hold a stack of books. It looks great, provides an instant library, and can be used as an extra seat when needed.

∾ Here's an Early American trick: punch holes in your own design in a paper lampshade to cast wonderful patterns on the walls at night.

119

❧ Serene ❧

❧ If your bedroom needs more natural light, hang a mirror approximately the same size as the window directly across from it. This will create the impression of two windows and will increase the amount of light in your bedroom.

❧ Hang a beautiful silk kimono or a pretty embroidered shawl on the wall as a piece of artwork.

❧ Keep a lot of scented candles around and light them at night for instant atmosphere.

❧ Hatboxes covered in simple white or craft paper are a nice-looking way to keep you organized.

❧ Silver picture frames collected over the years and filled with friends' and family baby pictures make a stunning grouping.

❧ A simple but large plant—like a banana leaf plant—makes a powerful design statement in a corner of a bedroom. Don't forget a plant light.

❧ Use a bamboo pole or a long, slender branch from the garden instead of a curtain rod.

❧ Place your bed directly in the center of the room on a low platform. Use the extra wall space as a picture gallery for your favorite photos.

❧ Keep your eye open for handmade Native American bowls. They are beautiful accents for any room, but they work well on a nightable to hold small bedroom paraphernalia.

❧ Splurge on a soft woolen throw in your favorite color and drape it anywhere you want in your bedroom.

❧ Pick up a poster of a favorite painting at your local museum, frame it in a clean white frame, and hang it opposite your bed for a refreshing view.

❧ Do you still have a copy of the invitation to your wedding, or to your children's christenings or bar/bat mitzvahs? Frame them in attractive gilt frames to celebrate the special moments of your life.

THE BATHROOM

Once a secondary player in the design of a home, the bathroom now receives considerable attention. As with the kitchen, a bathroom renovation can add value to your home. It is also the one room in the home where you can escape to be alone, to refresh your soul as well as your body.

Kevin and I lived with our master bathroom for over ten years before we were ready to renovate. Typical of much pre–World War II construction, it was a small, slightly claustrophobic room, linked to our bedroom by a cramped dressing room. As I explained in the introduction to my book *Bathrooms,* when I considered our renovation, I dreamed of being able to lie in the bath in the evening and gaze out at the moon and the stars. That was number one on my wish list.

My husband, on the other hand, had more practical needs, such as a shower with a built-in mirrored shaving niche and plenty of shelf space. And, of course, efficiency combined with style was paramount since, although time might be suspended for me during my evening bath, time was of the utmost importance in the morning with both of us trying to get ready before racing out the door.

My first step was to do some research. I paged through magazines and books, talked to craftspeople and merchants, picked the brains of my designer friends (and checked out their bathrooms), and priced fixtures and materials. I next consulted with an experienced contractor, Zoltan Horvath, who not only listened patiently to my dreams and needs but came up with some suggestions of his own.

He recommended taking down the door between our bathroom and the tiny dressing area. This would make room for a dressing table and allow us to have the three original windows along one wall, which would realize my dream of sitting in the tub with a wonderful view of the moon. He also uncovered enough space to install a small marble seat and steam-jet spigots in our new glassed-in shower, which was carved out of the seldom-used closet of our son's adjacent bedroom. This created a roomy steam bath without destroying our original budget.

I wanted a white bathroom because white is very soothing and serene and because you know when it's clean! And so pure white is found throughout the room, in thick towels, small area rugs, tub, toilet, and sink, toothbrush and cup holders, candles, and my favorite bar of Ivory soap. Cream-colored marble lines the floor and tub, providing a neutral and durable backdrop. Old black-and-white photographs, a dressing table I found on the street, and a few fresh flowers or ferns complete our master bath.

I love pedestal sinks because they have an Old World look. Since our bathroom still isn't very big, I also felt that a pedestal sink would take up less space. The one I chose takes up relatively little room, avoids the boxy look of some vanity-style sinks, and adds an attractive element to the bathroom. Since I was completely redoing our bathroom, I also decided on using the same brand and style for our toilet. I'm really pleased with the final look—and with the practical benefits of these fixtures.

Here's a fascinating fact: over 45 percent of women in this country declare that their favorite way to relax is by taking a bath! I'll be the first to admit that after a stressful day, nothing beats slipping into a hot bubble bath with just a lighted candle and a little music or a magazine.

But what really makes my bathroom work for me is that it has an organized makeup and grooming area. I'm constantly on the lookout for the perfect containers for all those new products I find myself buying. Just when I've organized my stuff in a set of pretty, round baskets, I'll find myself staring at some architectural-looking white plastic boxes at the hardware store, and I'll think, That's it! As long as I continue to buy new lipsticks, lotions, and bath oils, I'll probably continue to look for the perfect organizers!

These days I can't keep my children out of this bathroom and in their own, so I know I've done something right. And when I do get the room to myself for a long, leisurely bath, I realize how much I love—and need—this space, which fulfills my own personal wish list for a dream bathroom.

THE BASIC PRINCIPLES

Designing your bathroom is a challenge, but I've found that if you keep your eye on the end result, it can actually be fun and rewarding. Here are some basic guidelines for accomplishing this.

∾ **Safety** No matter how you design your bathroom, you want it to be an utterly safe environment. Steamy surfaces, slippery bars of soap, and stepping in and out of a wet tub can all result in serious accidents. When purchasing materials for your bathroom, be sure to specify slip-resistant flooring and surfacing in the tub and shower area. In our bathrooms, even though I used marble on the floor, I securely anchored the scatter rugs with nonslip padding to provide us with sure footing.

Excellent lighting as well as proper places to rest soap and other bathing items will also prevent mishaps. Another good idea is to install a grab bar in the shower and tub area. Even though you may not think you need it, a bar provides a secure grip for children, the elderly, and even for yourself while bathing young children.

128

❧ **Fixtures** Select fixtures that will allow for easy cleanup and maintenance. I chose white as the uniform color for all my fixtures because it's a soothing backdrop, it makes the narrow room seem larger, and I can always tell when it's squeaky clean. Also, be sure that enough room is left around the fixtures. The National Kitchen and Bath Association recommends 15 inches of clearance around the toilet, 12 inches around the sink, and an unobstructed walkway of 21 inches in front of the toilet, sink, and shower stall or tub. This space not only allows for safer passage but also provides ample space to clean around, in front of, and behind the fixtures.

❧ **Lighting** Lighting is important in any room, but in the bathroom, it is critical. Ample lighting is needed to shave, brush your teeth, bathe, and find your way to and from the toilet, bath, shower, and sink. Consider the full variety of light sources now available for your bathroom, including recessed, spot, and standard overhead options. The three windows flood my bathroom with natural light during the day, but recessed ceiling lights and light fixtures on either side of our sink provide essential overall illumination. And big, fat, securely positioned candles are always in my bathroom. Of course, as Oprah reminded me on one show where I had placed candles next to the tub, be careful of your hair catching on fire!

∾ **Storage** As with kitchens, storage is a major concern in the
bathroom, where towels, soap, toilet tissue, shampoo, lotions, shaving cream, razors, cosmetics, toothbrushes, medications, cleaning supplies, and numerous other necessities all have to find a home. Medicine, cleaning supplies, and other potentially harmful objects such as razors must be kept either in a medicine chest out of the reach of small children or in a locked cabinet. Under-vanity storage is fine for linens and extra toilet tissue, but you could also use a basket, table, small chest, bench, or stool for storage. I like the way a stack of clean, thick towels looks piled up on an old chair with a pretty little basket of soap on top.

∾ **Extra touches** There are many unique ways to change the look of a bathroom without going full tilt for a complete overhaul or renovation. So if you're feeling a bit bored with your bathroom, you might want to add a moisture-loving plant like a fern, securely place a small rug on the floor, buy some new containers or baskets for towels and other necessities, or hang some framed posters (just be sure your ventilation is good), and voilà! You've got a fresh look!

CHOOSING THE PERFECT SINK

The variety of styles, sizes, and materials for sinks available today can discourage and confuse even the hardiest of shoppers. So before you set forth, take the time to carefully examine your needs. Here are some important factors to consider.

∾ **Storage** Many of us use the under-sink area to store bathroom needs, such as extra towels, soap, cleaning supplies, toilet tissue, and toiletries. If this is true in your home, a sink nestled in a vanity is the right choice for you. The cabinet serves as a support for the sink and at the same time keeps your bathroom paraphernalia organized and out of sight. Another alternative is to use a wall-mounted or pedestal sink and skirt the base with fabric to provide storage space. If you have other storage space such as a closet or a chest, do consider a pedestal-style sink; it will add a graceful look to any bathroom.

    ❧ **Style** Sinks come in a multitude of styles, colors, finishes, and materials. Select one that works best with your tub, toilet, and shower stall. If you live in an older home, many companies now produce sinks based on traditional designs that work wonderfully with older tubs and toilets. You can also buy salvaged sinks from antiques dealers, flea markets, garage sales, and architectural salvage yards. Check the Yellow Pages or Chamber of Commerce for more information.

    ❧ **Usage** Some people use the bathroom sink simply to brush their teeth and wash their hands. Others use it to shave, shampoo their hair, launder fine lingerie, and even bathe the dog. Consider how you use your bathroom and look for a sink that will satisfy all your needs. Don't forget to carefully measure the space in your bathroom to make sure that whatever model you buy will fit comfortably. Too large a sink in a small bathroom not only looks unsightly but can be a safety hazard.

NEW WAYS TO STORE TOWELS

Every bathroom needs a good place to store towels and other bath linens. The usual solutions, such as towel bars, under-sink vanities, and linen closets, are fine, but you might want to try one or two new ideas to give your bathroom a bit of personality.

Try stacking linens on a chair, bench, or stool, for example. A pile of neatly folded towels on a chair not only makes a nice design statement but also lets you know at a glance how soon you need to do laundry. And it makes it easy to find a fresh towel when you or a guest needs one.

You can also store rolled-up towels in a large wicker or wooden basket and simply place it on the floor. Recently on *Oprah,* I used towels in two

different colors, rolled them into tight logs, and placed them ends-up in a good-looking basket. It made a terrific decorative accent as well as a handy and compact storage solution. You can also roll up hand towels and set them in a small basket for your powder room.

 A row of simple wooden coat hooks, each hung with a bath towel, creates a Shaker-like design statement in a bathroom. It also keeps everyone's towel separate and at hand.

 If space allows, an old scrub pine chest or a small mahogany dresser can be a wonderful accent piece for the bathroom as well as a great spot to store towels and other bathing essentials. Look for a piece with drawers, cupboards, and shelves to keep needed items accessible but hidden, if you like a clutter-free look.

 You might also consider neatly and openly displaying your towels on glass or wooden shelves. This is especially attractive if you have brightly colored, plush towels.

133

Creating a Terry-Cloth Stool

A great accessory for the bathroom is a stool to sit on while blow-drying your hair, waiting for your tub to fill, or applying a coat of nail polish. It also can hold your robe or book while you're taking a bath, and it will provide a convenient place to pile a stack of towels when you have company.

Stools are easily found in a variety of styles, shapes, heights, and materials, at garage sales, flea markets, and unfinished furniture stores. You might even find one stored in your basement or attic.

You can simply paint or finish your stool any way you wish. If you choose a metal stool, be sure to give it a primer coat of a rust-resistant paint. For wooden stools, a semigloss or enamel paint works best in the bathroom's humid conditions.

134

To create a seat that is specifically designed for the bathroom, make your own terry-cloth bathroom stool. First, cover the seat of a simple stool with polyester batting. Carefully wrap the batting over the edges and attach it underneath with a staple gun. Then cover the batting with thick terry cloth and attach, using the staple gun.

You can buy terry cloth by the yard at a fabric store, but a bath towel will serve just as well. Lay the fabric over the seat and cut out the shape of the seat, leaving enough fabric to wrap over the edges and attach underneath.

For a more customized look, use a monogrammed or appliquéd towel. Be certain to carefully position the monogram or appliqué before you cut the fabric. Now you have a stylish stool that's perfect for your bathroom.

STYLE TIPS FOR YOUR BATHROOM

❧ Romantic ❧

❧ Place your favorite bath beads or cotton balls in an old covered candy dish or some other covered container and display it on top of your toilet tank or on a shelf.

❧ Use pretty tea towels or small fingertip towels picked up from a garage sale or antique shop as hand towels.

❧ Hang a small shelf on the wall and display a collection of beautiful perfume bottles.

❧ Place a small bowl of potpourri on a shelf or flat surface where it will not be in the way. The heat and humidity from the shower will constantly release your favorite scent into the air.

❧ Find a piece of silk or some other soft fabric about 25 inches wide and long enough to curve across your window. Swag it across the top of your bathroom window and use rubber bands to shape the ends into small rosettes. Then attach the rosettes to the wall by hanging them onto long nails.

❧ Use a silver toast rack as a face cloth holder.

❧ Find a small Oriental or prayer rug and place it next to your tub for a unique bath mat.

- Look for an antique glove holder—it makes a great towel holder.
- Tuck favorite letters, invitations, and postcards around your sink mirror.
- Hang a vintage nightgown on a brass hook as a work of art.

❧ **Adventurous** ❧

- Keep a small magazine rack or bookshelf filled with your favorite reading material to enjoy while taking a bath.
- Paper the bathroom walls with topographical maps or nautical charts of places you'd like to visit someday, or place a few in simple but attractive frames.
- Hang a curtain rod or wooden dowel over your window frame, and swag an exotic-patterned fabric—something tropical, perhaps—across the top and let it fall simply down one side.
- Using a bit of raffia, tie a small bunch of eucalyptus sprigs to a press-on hook on the back of your bathroom door. The heat and humidity will release the wonderful natural scent.
- Look in secondhand shops for a small, handsome trunk—one with tour and travel labels would be wonderful!—to hold your towel supply.

~ Keep a spare, luxurious terry-cloth robe on an extra hook for overnight guests.

~ Place a small porcelain tray or oblong dish on your sink ledge or on the back of the toilet to hold your perfume bottles, hairbrush, and other necessities.

~ Place a rattan fishing basket on the floor in a corner as a hamper.

~ Shells collected on a favorite beach can be glued to a mirror or window frame with a hot glue gun.

~ Try a fancy window curtain treatment in your bathroom. One of my old living room drapes got a second life in our master bath.

~ Drape a favorite necklace (or a child's handmade necklace, as I did) over a dressing table mirror.

~ Use hatboxes as portable storage for all your bath-cleaning paraphernalia.

~ Keep a basket or bowl of plastic or rubber toys by the side of the tub to delight children of all ages. Don't forget to include a rubber duckie!

ॐ   You can often find colorful old ashtrays at flea markets and secondhand shops. They make great soap dishes.

ॐ   Store extra rolls of toilet paper in a nice straw basket on the floor.

ॐ Contemporary ॐ

ॐ   Use laboratory or medical containers to store bath essentials like cotton balls, cotton swabs, and bath salts. The chrome tops keep the contents moisture-free, and the glass containers look great.

ॐ   Attach a big stainless-steel bolt instead of the standard coat hook on the back of your bathroom door for a bold accent.

ॐ   Keep all bath essentials in a large metal basket; store it at the bottom of your linen closet.

ॐ   Silver trophies, baby cups, and the like make stylish storage for bath paraphernalia.

ॐ   Why not pick all white for your towels, area rugs, containers, and soaps?

ॐ   A sleek metal filing cabinet, coated with rust-resistant paint, can hold all your bathing needs and bath linens.

139

∽ Build a narrow floor-to-ceiling cabinet about eight inches wide to hold a selection of favorite reading matter.

∽ Place your facial cleansers in sleek, simple glass bottles.

∽ Traditional ∽

∽ Start a collection of small gilt mirrors and hang them close together on one wall.

∽ Collect old tin tea caddies and use them to store extra soaps.

∽ Remove the door of your medicine cabinet and in its place attach a gilt-framed mirror for a stylish front.

∽ Use a small bamboo table to hold hand towels and soaps for your powder room.

∽ Put a fresh toothbrush, comb, sachet, package of bath salts, and a small bottle of lotion in a nice hand towel. Roll it up and tie it with a ribbon for your overnight guests to use in the bathroom.

∽ Place a basket filled with natural sponges, a loofah, a pumice stone, and a bar of herbal soap near the tub to create your own personal spa experience.

∽ If you have good ventilation, hang some gilt-framed black-and-white postcards of favorite cities.

❧ For a touch of elegance, hang a small chandelier in the center of your bathroom.

❧ Keep your eyes open for old bamboo pieces and faux tortoise frames and mirrors for great accessories.

❧ Serene ❧

❧ Create an instant dressing table by draping old linens or some pretty fabric over a simple Parsons table.

❧ Create you own bath teabag by combining herbs, flower petals, and other soothing plants in a double layer of cheesecloth. Tie the top with a ribbon and suspend it from the fill spigot in your bathtub.

❧ Keep an ample supply of votive candles in different colors and scents, along with holders, in a convenient spot for those nights when you desire a candlelight bath.

❧ Buy a small bathing pillow to place under your head while taking a bath.

❧ Install a battery-powered waterproof radio so that you can listen to your favorite station while relaxing in the tub or showering.

❧ If space allows, store a small terry-cloth mat or floor cushion in your bathroom and use it as a meditation room. You're likely to get a bit of peace and quiet there.

❧ Fill a large ginger jar or glass bowl with shells, beach glass, and other favorite souvenirs from a special place and put it on a shelf where you can see it every day.

❧ Find an old bust or a stone gargoyle and mount it on the bathroom wall.

❧ Sterling silver–topped glass bottles make a stunning still life on a windowsill.

❧ Use an antique pillowcase as a topcloth for a dressing table. Vintage lacy hand towels layered over your terry-cloth ones can complete the look.

❧ Place a rectangular tray across one end of your tub and fill with soaps, oils, and a favorite book.

❧ Fill a glass bowl with lots and lots of sea sponges.

index

index

144